D0640957

pedro de la torre

JOHN TATE LANNING

peδro

louisiana state university press

De La Torre

Doctor to Conquerors

aton Rouge

WITHDRAWN FROM
WILLIAM F. MAAG LIBRARY
YOUNGSTOWN STATE UNIVERSITY

ISBN 0-8071-0064-1
Library of Congress Catalog Card Number 73-83909
Copyright © 1974 by Louisiana State University Press
All rights reserved
Manufactured in the United States of America

Designed by Dwight Agner. Composed in 10/13 point
Simoncini Aster by Kingsport Press, Inc., Kingsport,
Tennessee. Printed and bound by Halliday Lithograph
Corporation, West Hanover, Massachusetts.

R
558
.T67L36

To TATE, LUCY, *and* TOMMY

YOUNGSTOWN STATE UNIVERSITY
LIBRARY

344222

contents

illustrations

preface

THIS is not a book by a man too busy to write one, but a book that persuaded a busy man to write it—a highly subjective process that should entitle me to a paragraph or two of musing to explain a thing so unnatural. My original design for Pedro de la Torre was to write only a few paragraphs of his history in a book on the regulation of the medical professions in the Spanish Empire. When I did publish a few paragraphs—in an essay on the illicit practice of medicine in the Indies—my hope was that this roaming man of medicine would roam off and cease tugging at me with the suggestion that his story might tell more of life in a city of New Spain after the Conquest than might something far more ponderous. That he did not cease pulling at my sleeve, this little book is proof. It is not becoming in me to say whether the effort is justified. Once having given in, though, I had to find reasons for what I had done that others might accept.

For all those dour enough to require them, I advance

some such apologies here. So far, no historian has ever had at hand more than one of the three known files of manuscripts that, in the end, this miniature biography must rest upon. Moreover, every writer who has even obliquely touched this subject—and this is the only way it has ever been touched—has had an interest different from that of anybody else. First of all, there is the striking need to consolidate all the documentation on this exemplar of Mexican life in the generation after Cortés. This procedure should enable me to tell the story whole, and not in unrelated sketches—until, of course, somebody uncovers another file. Likewise, if my three biographical flashes are to be published in this country, they should be planned with the proper allowances for English-speaking people and written in their language. After all, the historical knowledge assumed in a reader whose mother tongue is English is about 90 percent different from that taken for granted among those whose father tongue is Spanish. It is not my ambition, much less my expectation, to instruct people abroad anyway.

To avoid unintelligible waxing and waning in the narrative, when De la Torre's story ranges off into that of Gutierre de Cetina, I have not hesitated to follow the poet while the doctor is left to sulk—as who would not in his tent?

If I have wandered off after Pedro de la Torre because it gave me pleasure to do so, I now acknowledge the debts I have contracted in this pursuit for the same reason. I should be more than remiss if I did not gratefully acknowledge my debt to the incisiveness of the late literary historian Francisco A. de Icaza and to the professional generosity and acumen of Dr. Francisco Fernández del Castillo, a man laboring simultaneously and successfully

Preface

in both the profession of medicine and that of history. My
debt is no less to Miss Rosario Parra Cala, now director
of the Archives of the Indies, for her searches in my behalf years ago and for filling in the gaps, whatever these
may have been. In the National Archives of Mexico, Professor J. Ignacio Rubio Mañé, the director, to the great
credit of his country has followed the enlightened policy
of allowing foreign investigators to make copies of what
they needed to do their scientific and literary work. And
while in that city, I should like to thank Miss Beatriz
Arteaga for watching out so competently for the interests
of my research in Mexico. Jesús Leyte-Vidal, doctor of
jurisprudence and Hispanic bibliographer in the Duke
University Library, has always dropped whatever he was
doing to come and advise me on points of law and procedure in Spanish courts, and he has often remained to sit
with me in silence over some sixteenth-century hiero-
glyphic until the light dawned.

To make the most critical point of this book, it de-
volved upon me to determine whether or not Pedro de la
Torre was "graduated as doctor of medicine in the University of Padua." For this purpose, through the intervention of my colleague Professor Ernest W. Nelson, I
enlisted the kind offices of Professor Giorgio Abetti and
Professor Cesira Gasparotto of the Academia Patavina di
Scienze Lettere ed Arti. In turn, and at their behest, Dr.
Elda Martellozzo Forin, of the Instituto per la Storia dell'
Università di Padova, put at my disposal her unique ex-
perience with the "Acta Graduum Academicorum" at Padua. Likewise, to assist me in this four-hundred-year-old
detective problem, Mr. B. Attolico, the counselor of the
Italian Embassy in Washington, put me in touch with
Professor Lucia Rosetti of the Archivio Antico of the fa-

xiii

mous Paduan university. The pincers that Dr. Martellozzo and Professor Rosetti brought together on Pedro de la Torre squeezed a truth out of him that the viceroy of New Spain, the *audiencia* of Mexico, and the bishop of Tlaxcala had never been able to extract.

Acknowledgments

Grants made by the National Library of Medicine, the Duke University Research Council, and the American Philosophical Society for a study of the Royal Protomedicato in the Spanish Empire have been of much indirect help to me in the writing of this book.

John Tate Lanning

pedro de la torre

prologue

EXCEPT for idle prospecting such as this, the historical bones of Pedro de la Torre of Logroño might have remained unprofaned for another four centuries. Yet there is too much about these bones that is instructive not to disinter them. Destiny pulled this curious character into strange places, threw him into the company of great men, and at last put him down beside some of the stoutest conquerors in all history.

As a boy, De la Torre casually admitted, he served Erasmus of Rotterdam as a page. For an alma mater he boasted both Bologna and Padua. He came to Tierra Firme with the *adelantado* Pedro Fernández de Lugo in 1535 when he was twenty-eight and was, surely, a companion of the Knight of El Dorado, Gonzalo Jiménez de Quesada, conqueror of the Chibchas and, as some would have the world believe, model for Don Quixote.

Once in America, he was everywhere doctor to Conquerors, taking them at cards and being taken by them. The "men's men" who had brought the Aztecs to their knees and their sons, both mestizo and white, were to him only casual neighbors. Juan de Zumárraga, the first bishop of Mexico, suspected like him of being an Erasmian, prized his learning and made a special intercession for him with Charles V. He, Pedro de la Torre, unwillingly vied with Francisco Vásquez de Coronado for the attention of the royal *audiencia* after the far-ranging and memorable expedition to the Seven Cities of Cíbola. The first viceroy of New Spain, Antonio de Mendoza, defended him as an hidalgo. He faced the episcopal inquisition when Martín Sarmiento de Hojacastro, one of the original twelve Franciscans who came to join Cortés, was bishop of Tlaxcala. He shouted—literally shouted—"Deus et natura idem sunt" when it was perilous to contend that God and nature were the same thing, especially for a man who had known Erasmus and skirted Lutheran Germany.

Beneath De la Torre's window, in a deadly fracas over his young spouse, two dastard sons of Conquerors cut down Gutierre de Cetina, the Spanish Renaissance poet so reminiscent of rare Ben Jonson. Both the poet and the doctor, when young, had gone to Italy—Cetina, the soldier, more on a romantic than a military mission, to address epistles, sonnets, and madrigals "of inimitable sweetness" to a princess; De la Torre, the physician, "to be called and named," as he said, "by dukes, counts, and other lords of Italy, Venetia, and Lombardy. . . ." What neither knew then was that they would move in the same path back to Seville and thence to Puebla de los Angeles where their paths would more collide than cross. What honest man could have touched so much fame as did this Pedro de la Torre?

Withal, he practiced medicine in New Spain with such lucrative success that he could establish two households and fill each with Negro slaves in less than a decade. Does

4

such a man deserve, or have to endure, the attention of history because his career three times flashes light upon the night of sixteenth-century medicine in the Spanish Empire or because his devious path three times crossed that of men better than he?

The documentary life of this man is a tale of three *legajos*[1] —one from 1545, one from 1551, and a third from 1554. As these three files of papers have brought light in reverse order, De la Torre's life until now has been merely that of an incidental physician either smiled upon or buffeted by fortune. It is a shame, then, to apply the first of these three records, because it exposes the hero as a fraud in the first place—he began to practice medicine in Veracruz with a forged license. Tossed not by fortune but by his own irascible nature, he was enmeshed, like an ancient Greek, in the destiny of his own character. That this impostor could yet maintain himself in public esteem and even in medical knowledge, beside if not above legitimate doctors, does not reflect the charlatan rampant; it reflects the scarcity of physicians in the New World. Quite fortuitously, this drama, in the last act, reveals the literal sword-and-cape atmosphere that prevailed long after Montezuma had extended his last kind greeting to the "fair gods" from "beyond the mists."

Because De la Torre's life, as documented, is like three clean pictures taken at night by three flashes of lightning, it displays the straits and the status of medicine in America more cleanly than any statistical table or any "social science method" we can now revel in. For escape from this alternative, let us be grateful.

---

1 A bundle of manuscripts, either tied together or cased. In fact, despite their length, some of these are merely files (*expedientes*) within *legajos*.

5

ACT ONE
ðoctor of paðua

TWENTY-FOUR years after the fall of Tenochtitlán, the *audiencia* in Mexico City fined the "said-to-be" Doctor Pedro de la Torre half his property and sentenced him to perpetual exile from New Spain "on pain of natural death should he tarry" in the kingdom when released from jail.[1] This sentence for practicing medicine with falsified papers, though in the literal sense correct,[2] gave more than pause to the surviving *con-*

1 Archivo General de Indias, Justicia, Legajo 199, pp. 13-14. Autos fiscales con el Dr. Pedro de la Torre, médico, vecino de México, sobre que no actúe en su facultad por no tener el título correspondiente. Hereafter cited as AGI, Justicia, 199. The pagination is mine, beginning with the title page as number 1.

2 Since 1528, at least, Spanish law had specifically forbidden any man who did not have a university degree in medicine and two years' internship with an approved physician to present himself to the board of king's physicians (the *protomédicos*) for examination. After that, he had to produce the certificate or title (*título*) issued by these examiners to successful candidates before he could begin practice. (*Nueva Recopilación* [3 vols.; Madrid, 1640], Libro I, Título VII, ley xiii.) Charles V applied this legislation to America in 1535 and made it a specific crime for anybody there to practice medicine or call himself bachelor or doctor without being grad-

6

quistadores, other distinguished residents, and even the bishop, the renowned Juan de Zumárraga. An epidemic of smallpox, alone destined to take off upwards of a million souls, was then closing down upon the capital. It was the culmination of two and a half decades of unprecedented mortality that saw the natives of Mexico die in untold numbers.[3] Moreover, for fifteen years before De la Torre's sentence, Mexico City had had only four medical men. Of these, one was no longer there, and one was in jail. The remaining two were rich and unresponsive, except to the "powerful houses"; and, one of these, when he was not sick, was threatening to sail for Castile. This was a ratio of physicians to population and to the whole problem of disease that was slightly improved but never solved in the two and a half centuries following. At every stage, the case of Pedro de la Torre is graphic evidence of this tragic and lasting want.[4]

Even more tragic and lasting than this want was the answer to it—the flood of ignorant and superstitious curers that flowed in as from a broken dam. The councilmen of Mexico City put it baldly in 1528. It had come to their notice "that many persons treat people and because they do not know what they are doing except to rob them of their property, they kill many and leave others to go on

---

uated in medicine from a university—all this the very year Pedro de la Torre sailed for Tierra Firme. (*Recopilación de leyes de los reynos de las Indias* [4 vols.; Madrid, 1756], Libro V, Título VI, ley v.)

3 Woodrow Borah and Sherburne F. Cook, *The Aboriginal Population of Central Mexico on the Eve of the Spanish Conquest* (Berkeley, 1963), 88, 157. These men estimate that the population of Central Mexico declined by more than 50 percent between 1519 and 1532 alone.

4 John Tate Lanning, "The Illicit Practice of Medicine in the Spanish Empire in America," *Homenaje a don José María de la Peña y Cámara* (Madrid, 1969), 144–59.

7

YOUNGSTOWN STATE UNIVERSITY
LIBRARY

344222

suffering the injuries and sickness" brought upon them "more by the doctor than by the disease." They then repeated that perennially repeated Spanish decree: that no one practice medicine or surgery without a license. To carry it out, they had all the practitioners, of whatever stamp, appear before the *alcalde ordinario* to show their titles in the presence of the *protomédicos* Pero López and Cristóbal de Hojeda "and to explain by what right they practiced." Penalty for disregarding this law: the stiff fine of sixty pesos.[5] The deluge of *curanderos* was so uninterrupted, however, that the city, in lieu of action by the king, continued for over a century to appoint its own medical examiners, whom it always glorified as "*protomédicos.*" Six of these served before the doctor from Padua reached the city.[6] Yet, these officers would not have dreamed of flying in the face of the town council and "the whole university of this land" to restrain Pedro de la Torre.

How like De la Torre that, after coming to South America with De Lugo, he quietly eluded the death and rigors of the will-o'-the-wisp struggle up the Magdalena suffered by his companions under Gonzalo Jiménez de Quesada![7] Perhaps his intuition for the easy course told him, as only the awful story of this trek told Oviedo after the fact could tell it, that "they would not take so much trouble to get into paradise." Where he was, in his time, no path could lead away from adventure. One after the other, he set up the practice of medicine in Santa Marta, Cartagena,

---

5 *Actas de cabildo del ayuntamiento de México* (54 vols.; Mexico, 1889–1916), I, 158.
6 *Ibid.*, I, 115, 158; II, 21, 30; III, 49, 61; IV, 154.
7 His excuse for leaving the expedition was that De Lugo died, but he neglected to add that it went forward under another command. AGI, Justicia, 199, p. 2.

Honduras, Guatemala, Tehuantepec, Coatzacoalcos, Veracruz, Puebla, and Mexico City.

For some years he remained in the port of Veracruz, where the unhealthful climate might justify a medical fraud. When his sham began to foreshadow his destiny, he cried that it was "envious persons" who accused him of being no doctor at all. The chief constable (*alguacil mayor*), Licentiate Alonso Pérez de Sandoval, did go before the magistrate (*alcalde ordinario*) in 1542 and charge that De la Torre, with no valid license, was practicing medicine and receiving pay from the inhabitants of Veracruz. The *alcalde ordinario*, Pedro Moreno, then took the simple route of demanding that De la Torre produce his "title" or cease the practice of medicine. As happened with all others who had practiced without a license, this one had left his behind—this time in Seville. He was, he said, "a graduated doctor" in medicine. The diploma he then presented to the town council, however, was that of a certain Dr. Molina, who had recently died. The vicar, Bartolomé Romero, acting as notarial witness, noticed that a name had been erased and that of "the intruder," Pedro de la Torre, everywhere substituted for that of the deceased—all, the harried man later contended, without his knowledge or consent.[8] Before he had time to reflect, he found his person in jail and his goods sequestered. The *alcalde*'s "definitive sentence," coming so swiftly, must have disturbed even his agile and accommodating heart. Said the judge: De la Torre, now out on bail, could not practice with the title he held and must produce an adequate one within a year and the license of the town council (*cabildo*) of Veracruz within eight days of receipt of

8 *Ibid.*, 5–9.

the title. As the doctor settled down to his long year's wait, he could pay the costs.[9]

De la Torre, the evidence is, resumed practice in Veracruz and hoped that the rancor of his enemies and the solicitude of the public servants would pass. Not so. "On account of a certain private passion" that Juan Dañasco felt against him, he found himself in mounting trouble; Dañasco was royal governor (*alcalde mayor*) and close friend of Pérez de Sandoval, who launched the "persecution." Now, two years after sentence, the remorseless Dañasco had taken a look at the trial record and made note of the tarrying tactics this said-to-be alumnus of Padua managed with such refinement. His ire now really up, he demanded to know what steps De la Torre had taken to meet the terms of the sentence given him two years before, confined him to the town on pain of two hundred pesos fine, and absolutely forbade him to practice without a license. De la Torre now presented "another title in parchment," and the *alcalde mayor* took his declaration.[10] When the *alcalde*'s man visited De la Torre's house, he heard that the defendant had hidden his clothes and effects to prevent sequestration.[11] This was the state of affairs when the canny Dañasco, who optimistically thought De la Torre had accepted his decision as final (*cosa juzgada*), had to send the case to the royal *audiencia*—the supreme court—in Mexico City.

There the defense did not improve. Viceroy Antonio de Mendoza, as president of the *audiencia*, and the judges (*oidores*) examined the documents from Dañasco and

9 *Ibid.*, 6–7. Sentencia definitiva, 11 de marzo de 1542.
10 His *confesión*, a declaration, generally under questioning, "not necessarily admitting guilt." Witnesses not on trial also made *confesiones*.
11 AGI, Justicia, 199, pp. 5–8.

had De la Torre, then out on bond, arrested and put in the court jail. The fiscal or crown attorney, Cristóbal de Benavente, accepted the charges made in Veracruz and forcefully advised the judges to inflict upon the culprit "the most drastic penalties" for falsely "calling himself licentiate and doctor of medicine . . . for practicing without a title," and then for presenting a manufactured medical degree and a doctored license.[12] Unfortunately for De la Torre, the dead doctor whose name had been rubbed out to make room for his was a graduate of the University of Lérida,[13] as the diploma plainly showed, and he claimed Padua as his alma mater. The result was a bewildering series of conflicting forms, dates, places, and names that the poor man's various *confesiones* simply multiplied. When the lawyers and judges, for example, compared the suspected "title" with that of "doctor Ximénez," with which it was supposed to be identical in form, they found incriminating diversity. Said the

12 *Ibid.,* 9–10. Dixo que . . . Pedro de la Torre aserto dotor que dezia e nonbraua en la facultad de medecina que se avia de condenar al dicho Pedro de la Torre en las mayores y mas graues penas en derecho establesçidas ansy por yntitularse doctor y liçençiado y curar syn thener titulo para ello contra las leyes e prematicas de su magestad como por aver hussado y presentado los titulos que en el proçeso estauan siendo como heran notoriamente falsos y falsamente frabicados [*sic*] por el dicho Pedro de la Torre por su mandado de mas de ser contrarios vnos de otros en el estilo y en los sellos y en las datas y en lugares cançelados y rraydos en las partes y lugares sustançiales segund que por ellos y por cada vno dellos constaua y paresçia en lo qual avia cometydo delito e delitos de falsedad de mas de aver contradicho y perjurado en los dichos y confisiones que le avian sido tomados. . . .

13 The fiscal had claimed that "if he were from that University," the enjoyment of a title from there was prohibited "by laws and pragmatics." Apparently the University of Lérida did not have the requisites for offering the "four completed years" of medicine. Graduation from a foreign university did not exempt a man from examination by the *protomedicato.* (*Nueva Recopilación,* Libro I, Tít. VII, ley xiii, f. 28.)

11

squirming man, in a louder voice: That proved nothing; such documents did not need to be identical.[14]

It would have made little difference whether De la Torre claimed he was an Italian who had come to Spain or, as he did claim, a Spaniard who had studied medicine at Padua. In those days, the answer to a man's claim to be a graduate of a foreign university, when the issue arose, was to challenge the claimant with the demand that he produce his diploma and license to practice. If this was not a method to encourage forgery, it was a way to make a fake tell a second lie: that he had lost his papers at sea. It was rarely feasible—and certainly not the custom—to write the secretariat of a foreign university, as would be done today, to see whether the claim to be a graduate was true.[15] So, an impostor could hope for some years of grace while he pretended to send for duplicate "parchment" and papers. The worst fate was to get a year's term to produce them; the best, to have the deficiency forever forgotten. Perhaps the royal *audiencia*, anxious to have another doctor in trying times, would vacillate properly. It did not. Instead, that body pronounced still another definitive sentence[16] upon the culprit. The state would seize half his property and exile him forever from New Spain—the exile to begin the moment he set foot outside jail, still on pain of "natural death"

---

14 AGI, Justicia, 199, p. 11. A certain "licentiate Ximénez" did bob up in 1538 only to be named by the *cabildo* of Mexico City as inspector of apothecary shops. (*Actas de cabildo*, IV, 154.) However, none of the witnesses testifying on the number of doctors in the city in 1545 mentioned any physician by that name.

15 The royal *audiencia* in this case and the episcopal Inquisition in a later one did not venture to ask him when the royal *protomedicato* examined and licensed him and, with his answer in hand, to write that tribunal to see whether, in fact, his claim was true.

16 AGI, Justicia, 199, pp. 13–14. Sentencia definitiva dada y pronunciada en la dicha ciudad de México en 28 de marzo de 1545.

should he linger. Yet, he did set foot outside jail. Because doctors—doubtful titles or not—were needed to cope with the epidemic then raging, the viceroy and *oidores* now let De la Torre out on bond.

Then, "speaking with all due respect," he told his stern judges that their sentence had unjustly injured and gravely wronged him. Indeed, he insisted in high dunder, he had been called by "dukes, counts, and other lords of Italy, Venetia, and Lombardy," and worked and walked beside the king's own *protomédicos*. Besides, for "thirteen or fourteen years" Viceroy Mendoza, whose chamberlain had known him in Spain, had had word of him as a practicing doctor. To this distinction, in a plea for revoking the sentence to exile, he added that in Veracruz he had an "inhabited house" and a wife—a wife then not over thirteen years old.[17] He wanted his enemies to prove their charges, not merely to assert them.

What, then, of the myriad contradictions involved in the altered title? All that proved nothing against him, countered the undaunted man at the bar. He had not forged such a paper, he had not authorized it, and he had not used it. The name inserted in the questioned document—a document that he himself now accepted as false —could be that of some other Pedro de la Torre, "for there are a lot of Pedros." Nor had he broken the law by calling himself doctor, for he was, he stubbornly reiterated, a graduated doctor of medicine from the Paduan university. The crown attorney spurned this thin defense. Viceroy Mendoza and the *oidores* reaffirmed their original sentence and imposed the condition that the exile begin nine days after the defendant received legal notice of

---

17 *Ibid.*, 15–18. In 1554, Leonor de Osma, the wife in question, swore she was twenty-two.

the new decision. Instead of menacing De la Torre with death for lingering, the *audiencia* fixed the penalty for delay at five hundred pesos.[18]

Then, between July 3 and August 5, 1545, the *audiencia* received as formidable a set of petitions on his behalf as it was possible to muster in Mexico. The town council, Bishop Juan de Zumárraga and the cathedral chapter,[19] an imposing list of Conquerors and other important citizens—"the whole university of this land"—flooded the *audiencia* with petitions. Then, in their responses to a series of questions (*interrogatorio*)[20] designed to reflect favorable light upon the direly needed but harried practitioner, Bishop Zumárraga, the Conquerors Pedro Guercio Valenciano, Rafael de Trejo, and many others[21] established some impressive points.

Most awesome of all, a "great sickness and pestilence which the lord has seen fit to visit upon this land"—a smallpox epidemic that followed the Conquest—was reaching its horrendous peak. In all the city and its environs, there were only the physicians Juan de Alcázar,[22]

18 *Ibid.*, 19. Sentencia en grado de revista, México, 19 de mayo de 1545. The signatures on this sentence included those of Antonio de Mendoza; Francisco Tello de Sandoval, the *visitador* sent out the previous year to publish and enforce the New Laws; Licentiate Ceynos; and Lorenzo de Tejada, the judge appointed to conduct the *residencia* of Francisco Vásquez de Coronado—a process then also under way.
19 *Ibid.*, 21–22, 24–25.
20 *Ibid.*, 25–28. The royal *audiencia* on July 20, 1545, authorized the town council to gather supporting information by putting this set of questions to witnesses.
21 *Ibid.*, 28–85. There were fifteen respondents altogether.
22 Juan de Alcázar, whose degree of Doctor of Medicine from the University of Lérida was validated by the University of Mexico on August 10, 1553. Archivo General de la Nación, Universidad, II (Cátedras y Claustros, 1553–61), f. 86. Hereafter this source is cited as AGN. See pp. 86–87, n. 96.

Licentiate Pero López, and now "the alleged" Dr. Pedro de la Torre. For fifteen years, witnesses testified, the region had seen only one other physician, "a Dr. Méndez."[23] Now, both Alcázar and Pero López were "rich and prosperous," and Dr. Alcázar was reported to be departing imminently for Castile.[24] When both of these disappeared into the country and towns surrounding Mexico City to answer the call of the great houses and rich *encomenderos*, no one at all remained in the city to answer the flood of deathbed calls.

Into this pit of woe slipped Pedro de la Torre, doctor of Padua. Just out of the viceregal jail, he was now lodged, by the grace of Bishop Zumárraga, in the episcopal palace. Nobody remarked, not even the bishop, that while bringing about the "many and good cures" that so many witnesses attributed to him, he was violating the very laws that landed him in jail in the first place. He charmed the bishop with his metropolitan conversation about medicine and "other things"—other things that make the historian long for two hours of retrospective eavesdropping—but he had time to treat and cure the bishop, who was impressed with the precise unfolding of his prognostics. Thus, on the main point of it all, "under God, and in truth," the first bishop of Mexico swore that he be-

---

23 Dr. Cristóbal Méndez, arraigned by the episcopal Inquisition in 1538 on suspicion of sorcery. (AGN, Inquisición, XL, Exp. 3.) For the particulars of this process, see Richard E. Greenleaf, *Zumárraga and the Mexican Inquisition, 1536–1543* (Washington: Academy of American Franciscan History, 1961), 117.

24 Why, asked the Conqueror Rafael de Trejo, would Dr. Alcázar want to sell his goods and go back to Spain, if he were not rich? (AGI, Justicia, 199, pp. 38–39.) Only Bishop Zumárraga, who had heard it from the Franciscans, mentioned that "Alcázar has been sick and still is because of the excess of work he has had." *Ibid.*, 30.

15

lieved the *audiencia* should lift the penalty of exile imposed upon his guest.[25]

Rumors—rumors that could circulate with almost electronic speed in sixteenth-century towns—for once worked in favor of Pedro de la Torre's reputation. To education and experience, he added an affable bearing and a humane disposition that made him responsive to Indians, Negroes, and Spaniards alike, at a time when there were not enough doctors to treat the rich alone. He waited with a lofty disinterestedness for his patients to suggest such a mundane thing as pay.[26] He treated the poor gratis or adjusted his fees to their means. He had come into fame.

It also "floated on the air" that, as the Conqueror Rafael de Trejo himself testified, De la Torre had cured his wife when her life was despaired of.[27] Another Conqueror, Pedro Guercio Valenciano, calmly but firmly stated that De la Torre had treated him for an illness that had hung on for ten years, leaving him greatly improved. Most curious of all, though, is that, along with bishops and Conquerors, Alonso Pérez de Sandoval, the *alguacil mayor* of

25 *Ibid.*, 28–33. Testimonio "del señor fray Joan de Zumarraga, primero obispo desta çibdad de Mexico," 21 de julio de 1545; Testimonio de Alonso de Aldana.

26 *Ibid.*, 33–34. Testimonio de Alonso de Aldana, provisor. Aldana, reflecting the view of nearly all the witnesses, testified that "al pareçer deste testigo a hecho en ellos muy buenas curas applicando para ellas muchos y buenos rremedios y diziendo el efeto . . . por lo qual este testigo le tiene por honbre entendido e sabio en su çiencia de mediçina e por tal persona convenible . . . y que este testigo por la cura que ha hecho a Rodrigo de Aldana le dava dineros, los quales el no queria y syn ellos le paresçe curava de buena voluntad e queste testigo a oydo dezir a otras personas quel suso dicho dotor de la Torre no es ynteresal. . . ."

27 *Ibid.*, 37, 60, 81. Testimonio de Luis Manuel Pimentel and Bernaldino Vásquez de Tapia.

Veracruz, who had first instituted proceedings against De la Torre for practicing illegally, rushed mysteriously to the defense. Indeed, and this may be the key to the riddle, the physician under sentence had treated not just the constable's wife and members of his household, but had treated the constable himself with great success, not merely once but a number of times.[28] Martín de Mallaybia was eager to say that De la Torre's treatment had banished a sickness of his that "the doctors of Seville, of the court of His Majesty, and of this city" (Mexico) were not able to cope with "in the course of thirteen years." Moreover, Licentiate Pero López, after observing Pedro de la Torre work, roundly asserted that "he was competent to practice in the court of His Majesty and [for that matter] in that of the king of France. . . ."[29]

Witnesses less distinguished than bishops and Conquerors exposed the neglect and special sufferings of Negroes and Indians in epidemics. López and Alcázar, in fact, refused to treat them.[30] Baltasar de Castro lost many slaves, he thought, because the doctors did not wish to pay them visits. Antonio de Oliver had just lost eleven that he thought a doctor could have saved. Though he had a contract with Dr. Alcázar to attend his household, in the pinch the doctor "did not wish to keep it."[31] Another told how an Indian slave of his, a silversmith by trade and "already dying," was "walking the streets" of Mexico, thanks to Dr. Pedro de la Torre. The realization

28 *Ibid.*, 65.
29 *Ibid.*, 69, 70.
30 It is not just that these men disdained the browns and blacks, but, as Bishop Zumárraga testified in Alcázar's case, they were simply overworked.
31 AGI, Justicia, 199, p. 54.

17

that the others could have been saved "struck him with remorse."[32]

This appearance of extraordinary humanity in the cry of the Spaniards for medical treatment for the poor Indians and Negroes—though there is no occasion to assume that humane feelings did not exist—has an economic explanation; the owners were simply losing property at a rate they could not sustain, and they knew it. Moreover, although the municipality had never hesitated to set prices for anything, including doctors' fees,[33] the epidemic in effect had put the doctors upon an irresistible black market. Baltasar de Castro complained that a doctor charged him 6,000 "maravedises" a day to go out of town, an "intolerable thing!"[34] Intolerable, indeed! At 365 days a year, the doctor's gross annual income would have been enough to hire an Indian laborer for 326 years. It would have stung his worship more had he reflected that the *oidores*, all but the highest-paid officers in the kingdom, got only 500,000 maravedís—690,000 under the doctor. When the time came, moreover, the professor of medicine got 74,600 a year and the professor of anatomy 27,500, a salary the fortunately anonymous doctor could have paid with less than five days' work out of the city. The suffering inhabitants (*vecinos*) thus took both of their doctors as "publicly" and "notoriously" rich.[35] Did not López—he of

32 *Ibid.*, 81. Testimonio de Bernaldino Vásquez de Tapia.
33 The *cabildo* of Mexico City set up the first official schedule of doctors' fees in 1536 when it required doctors to charge each patient no more than a *tostón*—half a peso. (*Actas de cabildo*, IV, 43.)
34 AGI, Justicia, 199, p. 64. Testimonio de Baltasar de Castro.
35 This conclusion bears out Francisco Cervantes de Salazar, who just a decade later in one of his *Dialogues* (1554), has Alfaro question a companion about the "sumptuous" house "that has a majesty I have not noticed in the others," and whose "delightful" gardens could be seen through the imposing "portals" of "chiseled stone." Zamora, the companion, replied that these mansions "were"

the fine house with the portals carved in stone—demand his pay in advance? Why would Dr. Alcázar, who would not visit the sick "unless paid a lot of money," be returning to Castile with his wife, children, and household if he were not rich? Why else had Dr. Méndez departed for "that kingdom"?[36]

The unanimous conclusion of the municipal council, the ecclesiastical chapter, and this striking roster of outstanding citizens was that the *audiencia* should halt and rescind the exile of De la Torre from the kingdom or, as the ecclesiastical chapter asked, do so until Bishop Zumárraga could communicate directly with the king. The town council had come forward with the reasonable idea that, because of the overwhelming need for physicians, the *audiencia* should allow the doctors already in Mexico to subject De la Torre to a rigorous examination and, if he stood up under it, to permit him to practice pending an answer to the proposed intercession with the king.

The *audiencia* would not budge. Every corporation in the city, surely, thought its decision literal, hard, and rigid. The suggestion, then, that a sentence signed by the

those of Dr. López, "now occupied" by his sons. (Joaquín García Icazbalceta, *Obras* [México, 1905], I, 87.) This assertion also shows that Dr. Pero López was now dead and that future references to a living doctor by that name are to an entirely different Dr. Pedro López, the man who founded the Hospital de Desamparados. See pp. 86–87, n. 96.

36 That Dr. Méndez had been arraigned (1538) by the episcopal Inquisition could possibly explain a distaste for "this kingdom" and a nostalgia for those of Spain. Dr. Alcázar, however, did not depart as expected, for he was still in Mexico when the university opened in 1553. (AGN, Universidad, II, f. 86.) He, too, was "struck with remorse" or saddened by the popular view of him; he offered, when the university "incorporated" his doctor's degree (also in 1553) to treat the poor free of charge so that "because of their poverty" they would "not die for want of a doctor." *Actas de cabildo*, VI, 116–17.

great Viceroy Antonio de Mendoza and Francisco Tello de Sandoval should be stayed while the bishop went over their heads, if anything, was calculated to stiffen the backbones of those already firm gentlemen. They still did not bow; their judgment was legally sound. They accepted the proofs offered by the city's fifteen witnesses "for whatever seemed fitting," ordered the scribe to give the convicted man a copy of the process, and said no more.[37] Then a curtain of silence fell.

Suddenly, after six months, De la Torre—in the hushed yet gay spirit of the-bridegroom-cometh—appeared in Madrid to herald his own advent: "I wished to come and give an account to your majesty. And here I am come. . . ." Here he was come, also, bearing in his hand, he said, his degree of doctor of medicine from Padua, where he had "resided and studied for thirteen years." Whether he recovered it in Seville, bespoke it in Padua, or reforged it in Madrid, he did not vouchsafe us. Here he was come, too, against the wishes of "the viceroy, *oidores*,[38] and the whole city" of Mexico. He could, of course, "earn a living here in these kingdoms and elsewhere," but "condescending to the pleas of the inhabitants of New Spain," he would return to that kingdom should his majesty be pleased to repeal his exile. He had "lost work . . . suffered great expense," and "left his wife there." Typically evasive in the beginning, light and almost tripping at the heart of it, this plea of his still manages in the end to evoke pathos. The file of the doctor of Padua, literally covered by this petition, came to rest in

37 AGI, Justicia, 199, pp. 86–87. Acuerdos de 5 de agosto de 1545 y 25 de febrero de 1546.
38 If Viceroy Mendoza and the judges of the royal *audiencia* wanted the "intruding" doctor to remain in Mexico, they did not contradict themselves by giving him any document to prove it.

Appeal from Sentence of Exile
Courtesy Archivo General de Indias, Justicia, Legajo 199, p. 2

21

Madrid on September 3, 1546, with two firmly bureaucratic but indecisive notations: "Wants his exile lifted" and "That, consulting your highness,[39] his exile be lifted."[40]

39 *Su alteza*, the Council of the Indies.
40 AGI, Justicia, 199, pp. 2, 3.

ACT TWO
god and nature:
man and inquisition

T IME told the issue even if the record did not. One day—September 13, 1551—six years after the powerful band that included Bishop Juan de Zumárraga had petitioned to save the "doctor" from exile, De la Torre is found not only back in Veracruz, but free of vexatious questions about the provenance of his medical titles. On the night of that day he had gone to a consultation with the licentiate Francisco de Toro in the desperate illness of the well-to-do Francisco Hernández, his old companion at cards. Licentiate Toro, reconciled to the worst, entered the bedchamber of the sick man uttering "holy words to help him die well" as De la Torre followed with a cross in his hand—more like priests administering extreme unction than doctors looking for a cure. De la Torre began on the soft note that the licentiate "did not have any conception of the illness" and continued with "abusive words."[1] When, at last seated in consulta-

1 AGN, Inquisición, II, Exp. 13, f. 361v. Proceso formado en la Veracruz en tiempo del Ilmo. Sr. Dn. Fr. Martín Hojacastro, obispo de

23

tion, Toro remarked that Hernández was so brought down by his sickness that nature could do little for him, De la Torre, not to be outdone, interjected with sustained heat and certainly in Latin, that that could not be as "God and nature were the same thing." When Licentiate Toro challenged him, professing not to understand, De la Torre, growing white with anger, advised him "to go study theology for twelve years the way he had."[2] As the consultation degenerated into anger and shouting, Dr. de la Torre stormed out of the house, carrying his javelin-like lance,[3] shouting "to hell with that yokel" and with the "ass who says God and nature are not all one thing." Only incidentally does it come out, days later, that the secondary character in the drama, the patient, is *ya difunto*—already dead.[4]

As the doctor burst out into the open, the vicar, the Reverend Bartolomé Romero, standing in front of his

---

Tlascala contra el doctor Pedro de la Torre. Confesión de Manuel Griego, Veracruz, 15 de septiembre de 1551. Dr. Francisco Fernández del Castillo has made use of this *expediente* in a short article, "El poeta Gutierre de Cetina y los médicos," I [Notas para la historia de la medicina en México durante el siglo XVI], *El médico*, Año 11, No. 3 (junio de 1961), 46–50. Other historians have seen it, some have used it, and one, at least, has noticed it as an example of the physician under the scrutiny of the episcopal Inquisition. See Richard E. Greenleaf, *The Mexican Inquisition of the Sixteenth Century* (Albuquerque: University of New Mexico Press, 1969), 103–104. The file has long been listed in the index of the Ramo Inquisición of the Archivo General de la Nación in Mexico City, where I myself found and photographed it in 1966 while looking for files relating to foreign doctors in New Spain. José Toribio Medina passes up De la Torre's encounter with the "primitive" Inquisition in a single sentence and does not even bother to cite his source for that in *La primitiva inquisición americana* (Santiago de Chile, 1914), 264–65.

2 AGN, Inquisición, II, Exp. 13, f. 363. Confesión del Licenciado Francisco de Toro, Veracruz, 17 de septiembre de 1551.

3 *"Lanzuela a manera de zagaya."*

4 *Ibid.*, f. 368. Confesión de G. López, Veracruz, 12 de octubre de 1551.

house chatting with a companion, could see and hear the man coming down the street upon them—angry, mumbling, and talking to himself: "He knows no more of medicine than somebody who never studied it." "Doctor," the puzzled priest asked, "whom are you talking about?" De la Torre replied that he was talking about Licentiate Toro, who had had the temerity to contradict him when he said "God and nature are the same thing." The vicar, understanding an heretical and pantheistic proposition when he heard one, thus softly but firmly rebuked him: "Dr. de la Torre, your worship is just a doctor; do not try to make yourself into a theologian, for you do not understand theology." Whereupon De la Torre, who had to top everything, held his ground by saying that St. Thomas Aquinas sustained him and that he would rest upon that authority. At this juncture, the alderman (*regidor*) Manuel Griego arrived and the heedless doctor rushed on to repeat and translate his Latin thesis into Castilian. When a mere merchant came up, scandalized at what he thought he had heard, and asked for still another repetition, De la Torre told him "this is profound stuff that you will not understand." For this excellent reason he did not propose to repeat himself. Such was the community of "honorable persons of good understanding" that was amazed and scandalized at such bold words and such outrageous "offense against God and our Holy Catholic Faith."[5]

De la Torre had that bold nature and touch of cosmopolitan experience that make a great hoax easier than a small one. Far from thinking of himself as an impostor, he had patently begun to regard himself as the prime intellect of all Veracruz and, of course, unable to abide the

5 *Ibid.*, fs. 360v.–61. Proceso contra el Dr. Pedro de la Torre. Declaración de Bartolomé Romero, Veracruz, 14 de septiembre de 1551.

contradiction of another medical man—even an "examined" one with a legitimate license. What he could not have foreseen was that his vanity would bring down upon him an investigation that would stir up every deviation in his devious life that was admissible in an ecclesiastical court. The interrogatory prepared for the examination of witnesses[6] made it plain that it was all but common knowledge that, in a card game at the house of Francisco Hernández, he had shouted, "Win I will, come God down from Heaven!" The rumor was running, too, that he had also burst out that he did not believe in God.[7] Far more concrete was the accepted idea that though his Indian maiden Luisa was actually his wife, he had, when grown prosperous, "turned about" to marry Leonor de Osma. This offense—"married two times" (*casado dos veces*)— was a never-ending plague of the Inquisition. What puzzled the investigators, but should not have, was that Dr. de la Torre, "being graduated as a doctor of medicine," treated patients "with words," mumbled while he scratched others on the scabbard of his sword.

The vicar could not have overlooked, had he chosen to do so, De la Torre's rash and scandalous utterance, shouted repeatedly in the presence of so many prominent witnesses. A month later, the priest and the apostolic notary had Pedro de la Torre arrested and thrown shackled into the common public jail.[8] That very day these same two went to Dr. de la Torre's house and listed and sequestered his property against the cost of the impending ac-

6 See the formal series of questions (*interrogatorio*) used to examine all witnesses presented by Miguel Blanco, fiscal of the diocese of Tlaxcala. *Ibid.*, fs. 407–409v.
7 *Ibid.*, f. 282. Confesión de Pedro de la Torre, 5 de noviembre de 1551.
8 *Ibid.*, f. 366–66v. Certificación del vicario Bartolomé Romero de la prisión del Dr. Pedro de la Torre, Veracruz, 12 de octubre de 1551.

tion. This Dr. de la Torre was resilient as well as bold; among other property, he now held five Negro slaves—three women and two boys,[9] none of them destined to reappear with the picaresque doctor when he moved on to his next practice.[10]

Pedro de la Torre now discovered, if experience still left him in doubt, that sixteenth-century durance was durance vile. As Veracruz was not an episcopal see, the vicar had his "quality" prisoner arrested and conveyed to the public jail, "well secured with shackles."[11] For his own convenience, as well as that of the outraged Dr. de la Torre, Bishop Martín de Hojacastro[12] ordered the prisoner, still in manacles, brought to the episcopal jail at Puebla de los Angeles.[13] A rapid, not to mention a secret, journey with a man in fetters forced Miguel Blanco, both the bishop's constable (*alguacil*) and prosecutor (*fiscal*) in the case, to take an oath from his prisoner that if his fetters were removed, he would not try to escape but go "straight without turning off or deflection" toward "any

9 Ginebra, Marta, Victoria, Sebastián, and Lucas.
10 *Ibid.*, fs. 373–74. Inventario de los bienes del Dr. Pedro de la Torre, Veracruz, 12 de octubre de 1551.
11 *Ibid.*, f. 367. Mandamiento de prisión, Veracruz, 12 de octubre de 1551. The certificate of arrest is dated the same day, fs. 366–66v., 375–75v.
12 Hojacastro, when nominated as bishop of Tlaxcala, humbly declined so elevated a rank until the vicar provincial of his order, the Franciscan Toribio de Motolinía, the author of the *History of the Indians of New Spain*, called him up to Mexico City, had him kneel in acknowledgment of his authority, and then peremptorily ordered him to accept the diocese. (In just the same way, Bishop Zumárraga, another Franciscan, though personally selected by Charles V, had accepted the diocese of Mexico as its first bishop only under the orders of his superior.)
13 In the years before the establishment of a regular Tribunal of the Holy Inquisition (1571), the bishops conducted all inquiries—the classic connotation of the word *inquisition*—and trials in matters of faith. Hence, in this first phase, the institution is the "episcopal" or "primitive (original) inquisition."

27

place or thing" on pain of suffering the penalties of "perjury and infamy" and of "the relapsed."[14]

There in Puebla, Bishop Hojacastro and his surrogate, Juan de Velasco, assisted in theological matters by the Franciscan provincial Juan de Gaona and the Dominican prior Jordán Bustillo, subjected De la Torre to a grilling that covered not only his headlong proposition, but all the rumors that floated in the air against the still beshackled man. What issued from this inquiry[15] is another chapter in a career that seems dreamed. Pedro de la Torre himself was the only witness he or the prosecutor could muster who knew anything about the career of this wandering man before he came to America. Since, however, the court record shows he was capable of falsification, there is nothing to do but to receive all his testimony with reserve. Now forty-four years old, "more or less," he claimed to have been born in Logroño, Castile. Given the contemporary victories of the Spaniards in Italy, his claim that at age seven he went to Rome with his uncle, a priest, is plausible enough. However, he offers no documentary evidence beyond his mere testimony that he studied arts in Bologna for four or five years—long enough to have earned his bachelor's degree—and medicine in Padua for six.

His examiners, betraying their fears, asked him whether he had lived in any part of Germany. His reply, uttered and heard without an inkling of drama, is astounding. He had lived in Basel—he did not remember how long—where he was "a servant to Erasmus of Rotter-

14 AGN, Inquisición, II, Exp. 13, fs. 376–76v. Juramento del Dr. Pedro de la Torre, Veracruz, 15 de octubre de 1551.
15 After this first phase, the bishop left the prosecution and sentencing in the case in the hands of his *provisor* (surrogate, or ecclesiastical judge), Juan de Velasco.

28

Page to Erasmus of Rotterdam
Courtesy Archivo General de la Nación (México), Inquisición, Vol. II, Exp. 13, f. 377v.

dam who received him as a page." But that, he hurriedly added, was when he was just a child. He had left Spain for Santa Marta sixteen years "more or less" before his present imprisonment and had resided in Cartagena, Santa Marta, and Honduras before coming to New Spain at thirty-five or thirty-six years of age.[16]

In response to a dangerous question, he grudgingly admitted that Vicar Bartolomé Romero had fined him two pesos for intoning in a card game with Francisco Hernández and Antonio Ruiz that win he would, "come God down from Heaven." Faced with blasphemy, he stoutly denied that he knew what his examiners were talking about when they asked him if, in the excitement of another card game, this time with Hernando de Espinosa, he had also shouted that he did not believe in God.[17] Obviously not satisfied with his answer that "no judge" had ever sentenced him, the inquisitors pressed him on a case instituted against him in Veracruz at the instance of Alcalde Mayor Juan Dañasco, a man whom De la Torre hated with a consuming venom and whom he still blamed for all his woes. He dismissed the whole charge with the bald lie that, at any rate, he had not been punished.[18] Only if he referred to some unknown case or was merely claiming that he had never been officially flagellated, could he have been correct. He had, in fact, been found guilty

16 AGN, Inquisición, II, Exp. 13, fs. 377–78. Confesión del Dr. Pedro de la Torre, Ciudad de los Angeles, 5 de noviembre de 1551.
17 *Ibid.*, f. 412. Confesión de Pedro Fernández de Burgos, México, 30 de diciembre de 1551.
18 *Ibid.*, f. 380. Declaración del Dr. Pedro de la Torre, Ciudad de los Angeles, 5 de noviembre de 1551. It was not the practice in an inquisitorial process to introduce a man's record from the municipal or royal courts, but the case recalled here has the earmarks of the one against De la Torre for practicing with a forged license, or, at least, one closely related to it and for which no records are available.

(*condenado*) and sentenced by both a secular and an ecclesiastical judge in Veracruz and by the royal *audiencia* in Mexico City.[19] He did concede, in his scheme of alternating weak admission with stout denial, that the proposition that God and nature were the same thing was not true, that St. Thomas said no such thing, and that he had had only some lessons in theology. At the same time he was emphatic that he had never married his little Indian Luisa.[20]

Though this case arose from a theological proposition extremely offensive to pious ears (*malsonante*), before De la Torre's arraignment was over it had strayed into medicine, for the Inquisition was ever on guard against curers who healed with words through the black art— necromancy. So, De la Torre was already on the alert when his examiners asked if he cured with medicines or with words and ceremonies. "Only with medicines," he replied, and "in no other manner." Then, the questioners wanted to know why, when treating people for the toothache, he asked the patient to press the tooth that hurt while he mumbled over and over "perli santima cali" and with a file scratched other words on the scabbard of his sword. His defense was that a sacristan in Seville had cured him and many other patients the same way. Naturally, he said, he did not regard this routine as superstition. He scratched words on the scabbard of his sword because this was a place to write; that it was an unlikely and inconvenient one he did not vouchsafe. When asked why, "being graduated as a doctor of medicine," he permitted himself to cure with the abovesaid ceremonies, he fell back upon his observations in Seville. More omi-

19 See pp. 6, 9, 10, 12–14, 19, 20 above and 35 below.
20 AGN, Inquisición, II, Exp. 13, fs. 382–83.

nous still was the charge that in Veracruz he had made a married woman come on certain nights to the house of Pedro Varela, "be with him," and then return to her husband's side "without his feeling it." He insisted that, contrary to what his examiners had heard, he had never enjoyed celebrity as a supernatural pimp. Neither had he any satisfactory explanation for the occult markings that figured on the scabbard of his sword or the mummeries that, upon occasion, accompanied his treatments. And, set up as a "Latin doctor," he must have hung his head when his examiners asked why he sought to cure a toothache by this means.[21]

The harried practitioner found the evidence against him as a bigamist hard to explain away. The witness Martín Díaz came forward to testify that he had heard from three men in Tehuantepec, one of them the *alcalde mayor*, that Dr. Pedro de la Torre, when he ran short of something to wager, actually bet Luisa and lost her "to one So-and-so [Fulano] Molina." Thereupon, he went before the *alcalde mayor* and took the position that he could not bet this woman because she was his wife. The *alcalde mayor*, after requiring him to swear to this assertion, returned the woman to him.[22] Miguel Blanco charged that in Coatzacoalcos he married Leonor de Osma and came to Veracruz, "leading a married life with the two of them together."[23] If one assumes that Martín Díaz' evidence was hearsay and therefore inadmissible, still De la Torre admitted that he had bet and lost the woman, a slave, but far from swearing she was his wife, he insisted that he

21 *Ibid.*, fs. 381–82.
22 *Ibid.*, f. 372–72v. Declaración de Martín Díaz, Veracruz, 15 de octubre de 1551.
23 *Ibid.*, f. 388–88v.

had neither married nor plighted her his troth. He had, instead, redeemed her with some "jewels and trifles." Later, he said, he had sold Luisa,[24] at the instance of Leonor de Osma, if she had the same suspicion the bishop had. His interrogators, on the other hand, had heard that he kept Luisa until she died in the same house with Leonor.[25]

De la Torre, with a confidence man's mentality, sensed that his fate rested upon softening his theological quirks. So, in prison, he immediately began to alter his story.[26] He cannily took time, in his succinct responses to questions put to him, to make it plain that he was a mere child when he served Erasmus of Rotterdam as a page.[27] Yet when Erasmus was in Basel (ca. 1521–1529), Pedro de la Torre was between fourteen and twenty-two years of age. Since the Spaniards expected bright boys to speak Latin and be ready for the university at the age of twelve, his plain intimation that he was too young to comprehend what went on around his master is not altogether convincing.

And plenty did go on around the famous scholar in those years. There the German printer Johann Froben gathered round his avid circle. Works—some of them immortal—poured out. Just over a decade before Erasmus came to Basel he published *The Praise of Folly* (1510) and now, in the midst of his stay there, came the crowning edition of his capital work, the *Colloquies* (1524),

24 *Ibid.*, fs. 382v.–83. Confesión de Pedro de la Torre, Ciudad de los Angeles, 5 de noviembre de 1551.
25 *Ibid.*, f. 408. Interrogatorio, Pregunta núm. 12.
26 *Ibid.*, fs. 369v.–71v. Confesión de Juan de Insausti, Veracruz, 13 de octubre de 1551; confesión de Joseph Juárez, Veracruz, 15 de octubre de 1551.
27 *Ibid.*, f. 377v. Confesión de Pedro de la Torre, Ciudad de los Angeles, 5 de noviembre de 1551.

33

both wittily satirizing the foibles, not only of the secular professions, but of men of the cloth, some aspects of theology, and the very church itself. If Erasmus' satire, especially when it rose to invective, advanced Protestantism and led the Sorbonne to condemn the man of Rotterdam as a heretic, it is too much to expect men as busy and as far away as those in Mexico not to suspect Pedro de la Torre or, for that matter, to distinguish very clearly between Erasmus and Luther.

And there is also an analogy, this one almost eerie, between master and page at Basel. Erasmus, born of parents "married in all but name," and De la Torre, born to carry forever only his mother's name, went off at the instance if not under the compulsion, of relatives to become novitiates in religious houses. Erasmus entered St. Lebwin's eventually to become a canon in the convent of the Augustinians at Steyn; De la Torre, under "the government" of his priest-uncle, enrolled in some nameless conventual school in Rome to go on, informants against him whispered, to become a "professed friar" somewhere —Rome, Bologna, Padua? Both exceptionally bright lads, they flourished as scholars, but both were too secular to find the life cloistral to their taste. Erasmus, capable of discipline, elected to devote his great and lucid powers to la Torre, incapable of discipline, took what John Bunyan literature and to the reform of "the queen of sciences"; De would have called the Road of Abandon, where, as is by now plain to all, he met Strange Fortune.

Now, faced with the diabolical heresy of asserting that God and nature were the same thing, the slippery Pedro began a wriggling course that his questioners recognized as diversionary. God and "divine" nature, he hedged, were the same thing, not God and "created" nature. His vehement assertion that he had never heard such a doctrine preached was tacit recognition that his examiners feared he was contaminated from Germany.[28] His humble yet careful admission that he had casually listened in on some lessons in theology was far from the twelve years study he threw in Licentiate Toro's face. Thus, by denouncing his minor slips himself[29] and stoutly denying his major ones, he hoped for a merciful sentence.

The charge against him that he was not a practicing Christian he found hard to refute. Did he go to mass and hear the sermons or did he sit, rapt, in a card game while all the world swept by to church? He went to mass and did hear the sermons, he succinctly testified, except on occasions "of lawful impediment." He calmly denied forbidding the women and servants in his household to attend mass, but he had to admit that he himself had once been fined two pounds of white wax for not confessing and communicating during Lent.[30] Not even his wife knew whether he had confessed this year—1551—though she had heard that he had confessed in Mexico.[31] Another witness had not seen that Dr. de la Torre went to mass during Lent and stated that his slaves—at least a majority of them—did not confess during that time.[32]

In a few days the formalities of the case closed inevitably around him. Yet, three weeks after his arrest and three days after his grilling, he was still begging—with

---

28 *Ibid.*, fs. 378–80, 387–87v.
29 *Ibid.*, f. 416–16v.
30 *Ibid.*, fs. 380–81. Confesión del Dr. Pedro de la Torre, Ciudad de los Angeles, 5 de noviembre de 1551.
31 *Ibid.*, f. 364v. Confesión de Leonor de Osma, Veracruz, 23 de octubre de 1551.
32 *Ibid.*, f. 364. Declaración de Domingo de Aldava, Veracruz, 1 de octubre de 1551.

hauteur—for an explanation;[33] the "quality of his person" and "his status as doctor" made his shackles not only unfitting but degrading. Besides, they left his leg raw and ulcerating.[34] To have these fetters removed, he gave bond through Luis Mancilla, not only to pay all the fines, costs, and penalties levied against him, but to post two thousand pesos *oro de minas*.[35] His chances of taking flight, however, were not good; his person was not removed from jail with his fetters. As utterly heedless in his speech as his danger was imminent, De la Torre now turned recklessly to his own defense. As he could not appear for himself, he petitioned Judge Velasco for permission to give his full power to Juan Ruiz as his defender, and if he refused to serve, to horsewhip him if necessary to compel him to do so.[36] The next day, two days after the date of his bond, the prosecution presented Dr. Pedro de la Torre with the charges against him—charges both sweeping and hard.[37] To De la Torre and his new counselor Juan Ruiz, these "were dirty, calumniating, and no true bill." Except that they roundly accused him of having picked up Lutheranism in Italy,[38] there is nothing in these charges not already clearly implied in the interrogatory.

33 *Ibid.*, f. 385. Pedro de la Torre al Obispo Martín de Hojacastro, Ciudad de los Angeles, 7 de noviembre de 1551.
34 *Ibid.*, f. 386. Dr. Pedro de la Torre al Obispo Martín de Hojacastro, Ciudad de los Angeles, 8 de noviembre de 1551.
35 *Ibid.*, f. 389–89v. Fianza de caución, Ciudad de los Angeles, 11 de noviembre de 1551.
36 *Ibid.*, f. 391. Dr. de la Torre al provisor Juan de Velasco, Ciudad de los Angeles, 12 de Noviembre de 1551. The words were ". . . aunque lo azote, porque no quede indefenso, e yo alcanzar justicia. . . ."
37 *Ibid.*, fs. 387–88v.
38 *Ibid.*, f. 387v. The critical words were: ". . . lo que el dicho Pedro de la Torre médico dijó es herético y malsonante y lo deprendió en Italia con el lútero y como luterano y mal cristiano a de recondenar la dicha proposición por herética y diabólica y el dicho doctor castigado por tal herético, luterano. . . ."

The outrage to De la Torre, however, was that "being, as I am, a person of honor and a Catholic, an hidalgo, an old Christian, clean in my person and lineage," he still sweltered in jail. Now that he was free of irons, he wanted the limits of the city as his prison. The only justification for his imprisonment, he said, was to secure his person—something entirely unnecessary with a propertied man.[39] And the interrogatory drawn up, surely with the coaching of Dr. de la Torre, for all the imprisoned man's friendly witnesses in Mexico City, was designed to show that his family in Logroño was of the class of hidalgos, a quality that should exempt him from the dishonor of reposing in a common jail. One witness even declared that he had heard Viceroy Antonio de Mendoza, who had just left for Peru, declare that the De la Torre family was noble.[40] And what a name to testify to nobility! Mendoza was of a family noblest of the noble and kin to more kings than the kings were. The only witness, however, who professed to be from Logroño knew less about the place, to judge from the internal evidence, than those who made no such claim. Though no trifling matter, it was secondary that they should testify that De la Torre was not the kind of man to go around uttering blasphemies but that, instead, he feared God, said mass and—prime commendation of all colonial physicians—attended the poor.[41]

Christmas in Puebla might accomplish more than nobility in Logroño. When, after seventy-three long days in jail and with the dawn of Christmas, Provisor Velasco, in "honor of the birth of Christ," released the prisoner—to

39 *Ibid.*, fs. 393–95v. Pedro de la Torre al Obispo Martín de Hojacastro, Ciudad de los Angeles, 16 de noviembre de 1551.
40 *Ibid.*, f. 426v. Confesión de Pedro de Salcedo, México, 21 de diciembre de 1551.
41 *Ibid.*, fs. 421v.–27.

make the whole city his jail—from Christmas Eve to Epiphany, December 24, 1551, to January 6, 1552. He warned De la Torre, though, that should he try to leave the city, he would automatically convict himself of the charges against him.[42] The more generous Hojacastro, the very day before the jailer expected De la Torre back in his custody, extended the liberty of the sorely beset man until such time as a contrary order might be issued.[43] Velasco, thinking it unwise to leave the prisoner at liberty when he pronounced sentence, ordered him back to prison "not to come out without his license" on January 21,[44] the very day he heard his sentence read. A month's freedom of the city was scant recognition of his quality of nobility, his condition as doctor, and, in reverse, the injury of his person.

The noble quality he had tried so hard to establish, if it got him only slight respite from shackles and bars, did in fact ameliorate his sentence. Given the age and the nature of the charges, then, Judge Velasco's sentence was not severe.[45] It fell into three parts. The first took the form of a penance, for it required De la Torre to go to the main church (*iglesia mayor*) of Veracruz and, at the time of the offering during high mass, to stand up in a conspicuous

42 *Ibid.*, f. 414. Licencia al Doctor de la Torre para que pueda salir de la cárcel, Ciudad de los Angeles, 24 de diciembre de 1551.

43 *Ibid.*, f. 414. Prórroga de la carcelería al doctor de la Torre, 5 de enero de 1552.

44 *Ibid.*, f. 435. "El . . . señor provisor mandó notificar al dicho doctor Pedro de la Torre que se vaya a la cárcel e prisión de su señoría reverendísima e no salga de ella sin su licencia. . . ." Ciudad de los Angeles, 21 de enero de 1552.

45 *Ibid.*, fs. 436–37v. Sentencia que dió y pronunció el provisor Juan de Velasco, 21 de enero de 1552. As Bishop Hojacastro had to be traveling on business of the diocese, he had turned the case over to his *provisor* Juan de Velasco to conclude (*i.e.*, to finish and sentence), f. 386v.

place and say in a loud voice so that all those present might hear that the proposition he had seemed to defend on September 13, 1551—that God and "created" nature were the same—was heretical and that St. Thomas confirmed no such thing. Only God and "divine" nature were one and the same. Moreover, he had to beg the vicar in the same speech to record his tortuous apology—all but a retraction—in the trial record. As if in a pensive mood, Judge Velasco interposed the summary order that De la Torre neither call himself a theologian, invoke the authority of St. Thomas, nor pose any propositions not in his profession and faculty of medicine. He then elected not to proceed against the doctor for heresy, for the superstition involved in the mysterious markings on the scabbard of his sword, nor for the "blasphemy against God of which he stood accused." Instead, he chose to accept De la Torre's confession, "without taking into account the contradictions in which he involved himself. . . ."

In the same mood, on account of "his honorable status,"[46] Velasco also spared the man of medicine the humiliation of the public penitence that could have forced him to parade through the streets wearing over his shoulders the disgraceful yellow sanbenito, with its red cross at the breast, as if he were exposed in a full-blown auto-da-fé. Rather, he fined him one hundred pesos *oro de minas*. Unimpressive as it is in an age of astronomical budgets, this sum was still enough to finance a chair in some universities for a whole year. One part went to the poor, another to compensate fiscal Miguel Blanco, and still another to pay the costs, especially of the elaborate

---

46 ". . . por ser la persona que es constituida en título y grado de honra. . . ."

notarized record. Banishment from the city of Veracruz for as long as the bishop wished was next. From this exile he might not "return without a license, on his own feet or anybody else's," on pain of major excommunication and two hundred pesos for the church and the Veracruz hospital for the poor. When he had satisfied all costs, and only then, his sequestered property would be returned to him.[47]

The immediate issue of this precipitate judgment was De la Torre's outraged appeal to the bishop of Tlaxcala. As "a doctor, a gentleman, and a person of quality [noble]," with "my sick ones" waiting in vain for visits while he was in prison, he "supplicated" the bishop.[48] The very next day Bishop Hojacastro commuted the sentence. Instead of reading his ready-made mea culpa in the main church of Veracruz, the "said doctor" might do so in the public plaza, in the presence of the *alcalde mayor*, the *alcaldes ordinarios, regidores,* "and other persons before whom he said those words. . . ." And with regard to the exile, the prisoner might have exactly thirty days—no more—to settle his affairs in that town and be gone.[49] For some reason hard for a pagan to understand, De la Torre saw mercy in this commutation, and, when he heard it read, he paid the charges levied against him and walked out of jail without debate.[50]

The *provisor,* on the other hand, turned testy; the particulars he drew up[51] to carry out the new sentence had a

47 AGN, Inquisición, II, Exp. 13, fs. 436–37v.
48 *Ibid.,* f. 439–39v. Suplicación del Dr. Pedro de la Torre, 22 de enero de 1552.
49 *Ibid.,* f. 440. Conmutación de la sentencia, 23 de enero de 1552.
50 *Ibid.,* f. 440v. Notificación al Dr. Pedro de la Torre, Ciudad de los Angeles, 23 de enero de 1552.
51 That is, instructions for Bartolomé Romero, vicar in Veracruz.

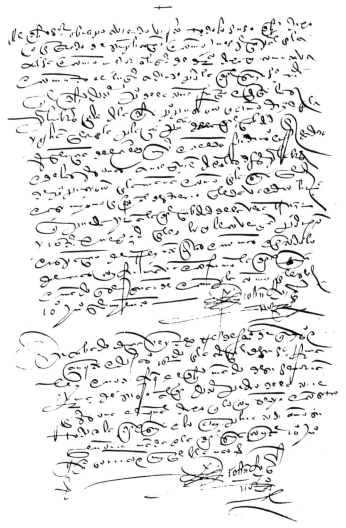

Bishop Hojacastro Commutes a Sentence
See Spanish-English translation, Appendix VI
Courtesy Archivo General de la Nación (México), Inquisición, Vol. II, Exp. 13, f. 440

personal bite. The occasion for the doctor's humbling was still to be a Sunday or festive day. Thus, "on Sunday, March 7 next," in the public plaza in the presence of the vicar and all the persons already indicated, "especially Manuel Griego, alderman, Francisco Pérez, and Licentiate Toro"—certainly Licentiate Toro!—he would renounce his folly. Recognizing that the recanter was a smooth talker, quite capable of impromptu sallies and asides, Velasco warned the vicar to see to it that the glib doctor did not stick in other words and discourses. The convicted man's thirty days of grace would begin the day he reached Veracruz.[52] The notary, when he certified the execution of the sentence, declared that many persons, citizens, and inhabitants of the city took advantage of this rare morsel of colonial amusement.[53]

As notorious as these sentences were bound to have been, they had no more effect upon the defendant's medical reputation than did his conviction for practicing without a license five years before. Two trials—one for forgery and one for heretical propositions—had done him no damage. In a matter of months, he was established as the leading physician in Puebla. This time, however, a fate so strange as to be imagined reached out and pulled him into the story of Conquest medicine and, willy-nilly, into that of Spanish literature.

---

52 *Ibid.*, f. 406. Mandamiento del provisor oficial, Juan de Velasco, Los Angeles, [borado el día] febrero de 1552.

53 *Ibid.*, f. 406v. Testimonio de Juan de Azoca, Veracruz, seis [siete] días del mes de marzo de 1552.

ACT THREE
ꝺoctoꝛ aꝺ poet:
ꝺe la toꝛꝛe aꝺ cetina

A MAN so bitterly accused and so decisively sentenced, one might think, would be content to hang his head and inwardly rejoice that he could go on practicing at all. De la Torre was of another stamp; he could never fade away for very long. In less than a decade, the "doctor" had passed through these tribulations and established himself in Puebla with a house, an entirely new retinue of slaves and servants, and, now that he had sold his "little Indian," with his acknowledged spouse, Leonor de Osma. This bold and idle woman of nineteen was to be the undoing of Hernando de Nava, a young ruffian living off the fame and on the means left by Bartolomé Hernández de Nava, his late father and a Conqueror who came with Pánfilo de Narváez to join Cortés in the subjugation of Mexico, "Pánuco, Tututepec," and many another place.[1] That this Leonor

---

1 Francisco A. de Icaza (ed.), *Conquistadores y pobladores de Nueva España: Diccionario autobiográfico sacado de los textos originales* (2 vols.; Madrid, 1923), II, 15–16. Hereafter cited as Icaza (ed.), *Conquistadores y pobladores.*

43

was not the undoing of De la Torre was owing to the Conquerors' pathetic need for physicians—quacks or not. This new explosion of facts on the doctor's nebulous career, after three years of silence, began on the first Sunday after Easter (*cuasimodo*), April 1, 1554.

Scene One
"They Have Killed Cetina"

On the night of that bloody day, noises on the street outside awakened one by one the household of Dr. de la Torre. Leonor de Osma, his wife, heard someone crying out, but "thinking that they were only some Indians and Negroes who gave those cries," she did not awaken her husband.[2] The slave girl Yseo heard someone in distress cry out "Oh! Oh!" but as she thought it was only "some Negro they were whipping and beating," she did not

---

2 AGI, Audiencia de México, Legajo 95. Proceso hecho de oficio contra Hernando de Nava, vecino de la Ciudad de los Angeles sobre pendencia en que hizo efusión de sangre, f. 77–77v. Confesión de Leonor de Osma, Ciudad de los Angeles, 21 de abril de 1554. This source is hereafter cited as AGI, México, 95.

Over fifty years ago, Francisco A. de Icaza gave a three-page but perceptive sketch of this 776-page process, from the point of view of the poet, and published, with commentary, twenty-two pages of excerpts from it in his *Sucesos reales que parecen imaginados de Gutierre de Cetina, Juan de la Cueva, y Mateo Alemán* (Madrid, 1919), 72–75, 219–41 (Hereafter cited as Icaza, *Sucesos reales*). Nevertheless, I am indebted to Dr. Francisco Fernández del Castillo for knowledge of the existence of this file. He learned of it from Icaza, who got his clue and some transcripts from Marcelino Menéndez y Pelayo, and he in turn was indebted to Francisco Rodríguez Marín for ferreting out or recognizing the importance of the file in the first place. (A footnote by Francisco Rodríguez Marín in Marcelino Menéndez y Pelayo, *Historia de la poesía hispano-americana* [2 vols.; Madrid, 1911–13], I, 27–30, n. 1.) Miss Rosario Parra Cala, now director of the Archives of the Indies, provided me with a complete photographic copy and assisted me in innumerable other ways.

44

"They Have Killed Cetina"
See Spanish-English translation, Appendix VII
Courtesy Archivo General de Indias, Audiencia de México, Legajo 95, f. 239

bother to get up.[3] Presently, though, there came shouts and a determined rapping on the door that aroused even the somnolent Dr. de la Torre. Going to the window, he saw it was Francisco de Peralta, who called to say: "Come to the house of Andrés Molina; they have killed Cetina."[4] (How ironical that the anguished cry of "Oh! Oh!" had come, not from some Indian or Negro, but from the mouth of the peerless singer of the Spanish madrigal!) After the servants opened the door, Peralta went in while De la Torre was dressing and begged him "for the love of God to come to see Cetina—that they had wounded him."[5] De la Torre dressed and hurried off with the distraught young man.

What was it De la Torre's wife and slaves had heard? That memorable night, the Spanish poet Gutierre de Cetina[6] and a companion, that very Peralta who had come pounding on the door, although it was already between ten and eleven o'clock at night, began what was, no doubt, the poet's last serenade under a lady's window. With their trappings off, they were whiling away the hour before bedtime playing and singing around the doorway

---

3 AGI, México, 95, f. 79–79v. Confesión de Yseo, negra ladina, Ciudad de los Angeles, 21 de abril de 1554.

4 *Ibid.*, f. 239–39v. Dr. de la Torre: su confesión, Ciudad de los Angeles, 10 de mayo de 1554.

5 *Ibid.*, f. 77–77v. Confesión de Leonor de Osma, Ciudad de los Angeles, 21 de abril de 1554.

6 Cetina, thirty-five, a soldier, and a wandering poet by his very nature, had gone to Italy, as had Pedro de la Torre, and then come to New Spain in the retinue of his uncle, Gonzalo López, *procurador general* for the whole kingdom. When attacked, Cetina had been in Puebla about ten days. His uncle had left him there when he came down with a fever and had gone on to Veracruz with a shipment of silver for Castile. *Ibid.*, fs. 33v.–34. Confesión de Gutierre de Cetina, Ciudad de los Angeles, 19 de abril de 1554.

of their inn (*posada*) not far from the slumbering household of Dr. de la Torre. Impulsively, they would have one believe, the two young men, instead of going to bed, decided to make a sortie into the streets, armed primarily with a guitar they borrowed, perhaps, from some loitering but musical Negro. Otherwise bearing only swords, they trudged in single file with Peralta slightly behind, playing the guitar.

Suddenly, as Cetina turned his head to say, "Isn't this the corner?" two forms (*bultos*),[7] as Cetina says, that seemed to be men materialized out of the all but impenetrable darkness, and one of them, brandishing a naked two-handed broadsword, dealt him a slashing blow across the face and temple that sent him reeling down into the mud. Just as he attempted to rise and parry blows, another dark "bulk" appeared and gave him a second cutting slash (*cuchillada*) on the head that felled him "like a beef," unconscious, nose down. In a moment, dimly regaining consciousness, Cetina could hear and faintly see the assailants hammering and raining blows upon Peralta. What he could not see was that Peralta, his belt cut, his breeches down, parried all those blows as he lay face up on the ground.[8] Neither the poet nor the guitarist recognized that in the darkness a third shape joined the first two in the flurry of blows.

7 Peralta testified to "two or three forms," a latitude that fits later testimony that Martín de Mafra, brother of young Gonzalo Galeote, joined in the hammering. *Ibid.*, f. 387. Confesión de Francisco, negro esclavo, Ciudad de los Angeles, 11 de mayo de 1554. See pp. 74–75.
8 *Ibid.*, fs. 10v.–11. Confesión de Francisco de Peralta, Ciudad de los Angeles, 2 de abril de 1554. Francisco, Nava's body servant, eloquently supports Peralta when he testifies that Peralta put up his sword to parry blows as the attackers laid on, *ibid.*, f. 285v. Confesión de Francisco, Ciudad de los Angeles, 11 de mayo de 1554.

Making shift to rise, Cetina, after falling to the ground once again, stumbled back to his lodging, where he found his companion Peralta had preceded him and aroused the guests. This comrade showed a wound in his right side just below the waist, inflicted apparently by a broadsword, a blow—not a cut—on the head, a gash along the right thigh that, with a Saracen's touch, cleanly slit even the lining of the trousers without drawing blood, and another thrust from the instep to the shin which, without cutting the pants, "barked" the leg and bruised the flesh. Those around the poet, who thought himself a dead man, responded to his plea for a confessor by bringing an Augustinian friar.[9]

Quick on the heels of the friar, but distinctly after him, came Pedro de la Torre and an old man named Antón Martín, a "chirurgeon." These two took a look at Cetina's wounds and declared that he would not live until daylight and, for that reason or not, refused to treat the poor man at all. Did the doctor of Padua know that the serenaders' design, and surely that of the attackers, was to play the gay blades with his young wife, something more than a coquette? What was more natural in that case than for him to invite a plague upon both their houses? Perhaps he remembered that he had begun the practice of medicine with a forged license, and perhaps he even sincerely remembered those gaping wounds with bone fragments protruding—even lodged in the eye socket—as, he said, beyond the power of medicine and surgery. De la Torre and Martín sewed up nothing, but merely put on some bandages and beaten eggs and tied them in place. De la Torre then returned to his own house, "leaving the said

---

9 *Ibid.*, f. 3–3v. Confesión de Jerónimo de Benavides, Ciudad de los Angeles, 1 de abril de 1554.

Gutierre de Cetina more dead than alive, for his wounds were mortal. . . ."[10] Here, in drama high enough for Shakespeare, is a doctor called to treat a rival laid low while singing under his wife's window by still another rival for a little more, perhaps, than just "one sweet look" from his wife's "blond, serene eyes," in Cetina's own words—the words of the most famous of all the Spanish madrigals.[11] To judge by the ferocity of the assault, the swordsman had long since scaled that balcony.

The next day the injured man sent for "So-and-so [Diego] Cortés to cure him by enchantment."[12] This Cortés brought with him an apprentice surgeon who sewed up half the wound on the face and lifted out two or three slivers of bone, but left one that ran across the left eye in such a way that it could not be taken out. And thus, after eighteen full days when he was at last able to testify fully, Cetina declared from his bed that he "was

10 *Ibid.*, f. 240. Confesión del Dr. de la Torre, Ciudad de los Angeles, 10 de mayo de 1554.

11 Every man who has enlarged upon the loves of Gutierre de Cetina has fallen back, as if hypnotized, upon this famous poem. Now, against my firmest resolution, I too succumb:

> Ojos claros, serenos
> Si de un dulce mirar sois alabados,
> ¿ Porque, si me mirais, mirais airados?
> Si cuanto más piadosos,
> Más bellos pareceis á aquel que os mira,
> No me mireis con ira,
> Porque no parezcais menos hermosos.
> ¡ Ay, tormentos rabiosos!
> Ojos claros, serenos,
> Ya que así me mirais, miradme al menos.

Joaquín Hazañas y la Rua (ed.), *Obras de Gutierre de Cetina* (2 vols.; Sevilla: Imprenta de Francisco P. Díaz, 1895), I, 3.

12 *Ensalmo*, a method of curing by mummery-like incantations and, upon occasion, by uniting these with more physical remedies. This sorcerous practice had long been forbidden by Spanish law and jurisdiction over it given to the royal *protomedicato*. See p. 97.

49

cured and is cured every day by enchantment. . . ."[13] The investigating judge then ordered the bandages removed, the notary certified that the wound running from the top edge of the ear to the gristle of the nose under the left eye was in a tolerable state, while the wound on the head had closed and seemed well.[14] This testimony is the last heard, in the process or anywhere else, about the immediate success or failure of this treatment.[15]

While Cetina and Peralta were buckling on their swords, but with no other weapons either offensive or defensive, Hernando de Nava, a foully spoiled youth, and Gonzalo Galeote,[16] a misled one, were girding on their own imposing harness. Both wore coats of mail and chain-mail trousers, while Nava, with a casque on his head, carried—at the last moment—a naked broadsword and Galeote, protected by a shield, dangled a sword at his

13 AGI, México, 95, fs. 33v.–37v. Confesión de Gutierre de Cetina, Ciudad de los Angeles, 19 de abril de 1554. Extracted and published by Icaza, *Sucesos reales*, 222–27.

14 AGI, México, 95, fs. 36v.–37. Certifications of "Doctor Gutiérrez," Diego Cortés, and the *escribano*, Juan Guevara, Ciudad de los Angeles, 19 de abril de 1554.

15 No one knows more than that three years later, Gutierre de Cetina was dead. When, on June 5, 1557, the outlaw Gonzalo Galeote petitioned for immunity from arrest "because he was not guilty" of Nava's crimes against the wife of Dr. de la Torre and the poet, he disclosed, in a single word, that the poet was "deceased." *Ibid.*, f. 387. Petición de indulto de Gonzalo Galeote, 5 de junio de 1557. Icaza, *Sucesos reales*, 241.

16 "Galeotillo," son of Alonso Galeote, who first came to New Spain with Juan de Grijalva and was with "the Marquis" in the capture of Mexico City, "y de las demás conquistas que antes della se hizieron, con sus armas y cauallo. . . ." The Conqueror Gonzalo Galeote of Huelva, the grandfather of Galeotillo, took part in the subjugation of "Española, Cuba, Puerto Rico, Jamaica, Tierra Firme, and many provinces of New Spain." (Icaza [ed.], *Conquistadores y pobladores*, I, 81–82n.) In 1525 the *cabildo* in Mexico City took "the solemn oath" of Alonso Galeote as "lieutenant *alguacil*" [constable] and gave him "the power to perform the duties of said office." (*Actas de cabildo*, I, 57. Cabildo de 26 septiembre de 1525.)

side. Nava, as a sartorial fillip, sported white breeches and a white hooded doublet.[17] Though they might suspect, neither the *alcalde* nor the gossips of Puebla were privy to this little scene. Much less could they know that in a little while, in a wanton fury that seems imagined to an eminent historian of Spanish literature centuries later, they hacked down Cetina and his musician and, while enjoying sanctuary, sallied out to begin a month-long rampage that terrorized the city and ended in the disfiguring of the loose, empty-pated, illiterate Leonor de Osma, spouse of Dr. Pedro de la Torre.

Every observer, after asking himself whether Cetina would die, pondered another question: Who committed the crime? In a place as small as Puebla with so few European inhabitants, no such outrage could long remain a mystery—even if a prosecutor could prove nothing. That Nava had wounded Cetina was, then, "nothing more than what they say publicly in the whole city. . . ."[18] Even while De la Torre was examining the patient, the young man, twenty-year-old Gonzalo Galeote, arrived carrying a two-handed broadsword and wearing a black damask cloak to ask anxiously: "Is this a mortal wound?" Dr. de la Torre, suspecting the cause of this intense interest, asked Galeote why he wanted to know. When the young man replied that it was very important to him, De la Torre shot back: "I swear to God you did it or you would not ask me this."

Besides, later, upon the arrival of the investigating judge in town, Galeote went to De la Torre's house and

---

17 AGI, México, 95, f. 286. Confesión de Francisco, negro esclavo, Ciudad de los Angeles, 11 de mayo de 1554.
18 *Ibid.*, f. 78. Confesión de Leonor de Osma, Ciudad de los Angeles, 21 de abril de 1554.

said: "Señor doctor, for the love of God find out if there is a warrant out for me, as I was the one who gave Cetina the gash in the head and I have his hat in my possession. . . ." Then, he rushed on to say, he himself gave Peralta seven or eight slashes and could not understand why they had not wounded him. De la Torre, accurately reading this nervousness, "held it for certain" that Nava and Galeote "gave the said gashes to Cetina."

The day after this shocking onslaught upon the poet, De la Torre had gone to the house of Catalina Vélez Rascón to treat her daughter Ana de Nava, wife of San Juan de Zúñiga. There he heard this whole family say that as soon as Hernando de Nava, son of Catalina Vélez Rascón, was secure, "something would have to be done, for they acknowledged that Hernando had inflicted those cuts. . . ."[19]

In a case such as this, touching that indefinable honor of the sixteenth-century Spaniards, documents, unless they are put together imaginatively, after all the innuendos and asides, can lead at best to frustration and at worst to schizophrenia. Instead, after gazing into this caldron of human nature and without dancing around it once, the historian must conjure up the only picture he is going to see. Nava was intimate with Madame de la Torre and so in some degree was Francisco de Peralta. After all, Madame de la Torre was twenty-five years younger than her husband and, besides, she could have had no respect for his fidelity. She knew this forty-seven-year-old spouse either for a fornicator or a bigamist, if not both. Moreover, she could have had a hand in forcing him to get his "little Indian" out of her house. The *señora* herself, il-

19 *Ibid.*, f. 231. Dr. de la Torre, su confesión, Ciudad de los Angeles, 10 de mayo de 1554.

literate as was her grandmother,[20] was certainly hare-brained. Nava was near her own age, mean, utterly thoughtless, and reckless beyond belief. His companion, young Galeote, only twenty, was his bewitched and servile Jonathan.

On the other hand, Peralta was more urbane, a man of the world capable of carrying off his amours not only with success but with discretion. His relation with this temptress could hardly have been so sordid nor, in eleven short days, his opportunities so extensive as to permit him to introduce the lodger Gutierre de Cetina into the De la Torre house as he might into a bordello. For him to pass by that house in the role of pander, playing a guitar, with his customer Cetina a little ahead of him, is too much. Since the poet, now recovered from his fever, was merely waiting for his uncle Gonzalo López to return from Veracruz, eleven days' time was too short for these two men, even if they were very congenial, to have formed more than a casual friendship; unless, as Rodríguez Marín erroneously states,[21] Peralta had been left at the lodge by Cetina's uncle to look after and keep his nephew company. This figment, too, is from the imagination, for Peralta was not only well established in his amorous adventure with Leonor de Osma de la Torre, but he actually lived in Puebla next to the house of Lázaro de la Roca, where he had his trysting place with her.[22] The acquain-

---

20 AGN, Inquisición, II, Exp. 13, f. 365. "No firmo la dicha Leonor de Osma dijo no saber. . . ." (Veracruz, 23 de octubre de 1551.)

21 In Menéndez y Pelayo, *Historia de la poesía,* I, 27, n. 1.

22 Yseo, a personal servant of Madame de la Torre, swore, ". . . que demas desto este testigo sabe e a visto quel dicho Hernando de Nava a ydo muchas vezes de dia e de noche a su casa de su ama desta declarante e a hablado con ella y entre otras cosas le a rreñido muchas vezes por que a ydo e va en casa de Lazaro de la Roca *ques junto a vna casa adonde bivia un Peralta teniendo çelos del dicho*

tance of Peralta and Cetina, then, was precisely like that of Nava and Cetina—formed between lodger and inhabitant (*vecino*). After all, the European populace of Puebla was small and, beyond doubt, hungry for outside company and hospitable to it. Besides, in case of irresistible need, Cetina, like Dr. de la Torre himself, could have found his own "little Indian."

But for a single witness, one could mistakenly adduce, as Rodríguez Marín did adduce,[23] that, in the darkness, Nava first fell upon Cetina by accident and seeing his mistake turned to fall upon Peralta—his selected victim. This thesis does not run counter to quick and plain testimony that Nava was indeed jealous of him,[24] but Peralta's honor would hardly allow him to venture beyond his own business to involve Cetina, who had adamantly refused to involve himself. Moreover, Francisco, Nava's Negro waiting boy, without whose testimony this case would still be inconclusive in nearly every particular, has Nava and his companions conspiring in his presence and prior to the ambush to kill both Cetina and Peralta—without one note of distinction.[25] In any event, if Nava denied, as he did, that he had even left the house the night he waylaid Cetina, would he be so witless as to reveal what his inten-

---

Peralta, e aliende desto la mandava que no saliese de su casa ni fuese a ningun cabo sin liçençia. . . ." (The italics are not in the original.) AGI, México, 95, fs. 294v.–95.

23 In Menéndez y Pelayo, *Historia de la poesía,* I, 28–29, n. 1. Francisco de Icaza, *Sucesos reales,* 215, with much more reason thinks that partisans realized that, given the influence of Cetina, it would be "extenuating" to have the attack made upon the poet an accident.

24 AGI, México, 95, f. 11–11v. Confesión de Francisco de Peralta, Ciudad de los Angeles, 2 de abril de 1554. "Por la mala voluntad que tenia con el sobre una muger que servia. . . ."

25 *Ibid.,* fs. 185v.–86. Confesión de Francisco, negro esclavo, Ciudad de los Angeles, ll de mayo de 1554.

tions were? Nava was quite catholic in his selection of men to be jealous of, and Cetina's comradery with Peralta no doubt accentuated his insane jealousy. What compounded his perfidy was that he entertained the wayfarer Cetina repeatedly in his mother's house, took walks around town with him and, up to the last moment, showed no signs of anger.[26]

Hernando de Nava, if his bravado allowed him to reflect at all, had entirely miscalculated the legal forces against him. Rumor, if not the eyewitness evidence, was running so clearly against him and "Galeotillo" that on the day following the attack, Alcalde Pedro Moreno, who had started his inquiries in the lodging house the night before, arrested Nava and put him in the public jail of the city. One morning soon thereafter, when Dr. Pedro de la Torre went to visit Isabel Vélez, Nava's sister, who was sick, he found Nava there in a shirt and cloak of violet taffeta. Turning to his patient, he asked: "Do you not know that it is rumored publicly in this city that your brother Hernando de Nava inflicted those gashes upon Gutierre de Cetina and that Young Galeote [Galeotillo] was with him?" Hernando himself countered that the attack was made to make Cetina run and that if he had wanted to he could easily have killed him. Whereupon, De la Torre told him, "I verily believe thou art the one, or thou wouldst not say this to me." Hernando then kept his silence.[27] This singular admission, remarked by no historian until now and utterly unbeknownst to Dr. de la Torre, fits word for word Nava's boast over Peralta's

---

26 *Ibid.*, f. 45. Confesión de Francisco de Peralta, Ciudad de los Angeles, 20 de abril de 1554.
27 *Ibid.*, f. 240v. Dr. Pedro de la Torre: su confesión, Ciudad de los Angeles, 10 de mayo de 1554.

prostrate form: "If I wished to kill you, I could very well do it. . . ."[28]

When, on the very first night, Nava escaped from jail, everybody believed, or seemed to believe, that he had flown with the aid of powerful influences that, in effect, turned him loose upon the city. Indeed, Nava had dined with the bishop immediately before the sortie that brought Cetina down. Moreover, the first bishop of New Spain, a Franciscan seconded by Franciscans, had set the tone of church-state hostility by openly opposing the royal *audiencia* and by summarily excommunicating that body for violating sanctuary. Though that earlier *audiencia* was corrupt, the civil authorities could not but feel that the Franciscans in Puebla, where the bishop was also a Franciscan, were still antagonistic and capable of foiling royal authority. Though it was rumored, according to sworn testimony,[29] that the Franciscans were confederates of Nava in his escape, an eyewitness of that event who listed the actual participants makes no mention of them at all.[30]

Viceroy Luis de Velasco and the judges of the *audiencia* now dispatched the Bachelor Alonso Martínez to take charge of the case as judge-investigator (*juez pesquisidor*). Martínez summoned every man or woman who

28 *Ibid.*, f. 285v. Confesión de Francisco, negro esclavo, Ciudad de los Angeles, 11 de mayo de 1554. " . . . e se fueron tras del dicho Peralta el qual huyendo e le alcançaron e le dieron muchos golpes en el suelo porque avia caydo e ponia la espada delante y davan en ella y entonçes dixo el dicho Hernando de Nava sy yo quisiese matar vos bien podria. . . ."
29 *Ibid.*, f. 94. Confesión de Andrés de Herrera, Ciudad de los Angeles, 23 de abril de 1554.
30 *Ibid.*, fs. 287–90. Confesión de Francisco, negro esclavo, Ciudad de los Angeles, 11 de mayo de 1554. See p. 76.

could throw light on the case to appear and testify under oath. However, the arrival of the royal judge so alarmed the guilty parties that they fell back again upon their sanctuary. Galeote, in company with another man, when he was about to meet the judge-investigator face to face in the street, gave his horse full rein and went off at a dead run for the Dominican monastery. His weak defense was that, since everybody was saying that if Hernando de Nava had sabered Cetina, "they were bound to say that Young Galeote was involved in it too."[31] And all during this month of April, 1554, these young menaces, when they chose, dressed as friars, left the monastery, changed their clothes, took up arms, and went about their business—always nefarious. Even Peralta, who had committed no crime, had taken refuge from danger in the Augustinian monastery.[32]

Meanwhile, how fared Cetina? The surgeon Gaspar Rodríguez testified on April 9 that he had been treating Cetina and that he was also being treated through enchantment (*ensalmo*) by Diego Cortés and that, the wound being healed, it would be a false treatment to go on with the enchantment. Because the wound did not reach the temple, he thought that it would not be fatal and was not, indeed, very dangerous.[33] On this same day Cetina dispatched his first declaration,[34] but it was not until ten days later that he was strong enough to make that

31 *Ibid.*, fs. 59–60. Confesión de Gonzalo Galeote, 20 de abril de 1554.
32 *Ibid.*, fs. 42–47. Confesión de Francisco de Peralta, Ciudad de los Angeles, 20 de abril de 1554.
33 *Ibid.*, fs. 23–24. Confesión de Gaspar Rodríguez, cirujano, Ciudad de los Angeles, 9 de abril de 1554.
34 *Ibid.*, fs. 24v–25v. Confesión de Gutierre de Cetina, Ciudad de los Angeles, 9 de abril de 1554.

graphic declaration that would establish him, if nothing else did, as a master of his native tongue.[35]

There is a curious, unbelievable silence on the motive in this case. The magistrates without exception elected, contrary to the French advice, not to look for the woman. The slaves and servants in both the Nava and De la Torre households closed their lips. Among the gentlemen, a chivalric sense of honor came into play. When, in the first moments of his treatment on the night of April 1, De la Torre asked Cetina who had wounded him, the reply was: "Do not ask me anything at all."[36] Cetina's pre-Cervantes chivalry would allow him to involve no woman, even if it meant his base assailant should escape scot-free. Too sick to testify though he still was on April 9, Cetina told Lieutenant Corregidor Martín de Calahorra that he was disposed to answer any question put to him "so long as it does not prejudice my honor . . ." and that, in that case, he would not tell what he did know.[37] In his last declaration ten days later, he clung doggedly to this quixotic silence; he did not know anybody who was mad at or jealous of him. He might surmise who had actually felled him, he said, but he would neither prefer charges against anyone nor demand that justice be done in this case.[38] Nor does one word of domestic infelicity escape Dr. de la

35 *Ibid.*, fs. 33v.–37v. (misnumbered 38v.). Confesión de Gutierre de Cetina, Ciudad de los Angeles, 19 de abril de 1554.

36 *Ibid.*, f. 239v. Dr. de la Torre: su confesión, Ciudad de los Angeles, 10 de mayo de 1554.

37 *Ibid.*, fs. 24v.–25. Confesión de Gutierre de Centina, 9 de abril de 1554. The exact words were ". . . que esta presto de declarar todo lo que se le preguntare con tal que no perjudique a su honrra porque en tal caso de lo que tocare a su onrra no aclarara lo cierto. . . ."

38 *Ibid.*, f. 37–37v. Confesión de Gutierre de Cetina, Ciudad de los Angeles, 19 de abril de 1554.

Torre, who, except for his passionate conviction that Nava cut down Cetina, moves through the action like an automaton. Thus, when on account of his wife, he was called to treat the most famous poet ever to visit New Spain, he gave no more sign that his spouse was a harlot than he did that Cetina was a poet.[39]

Even Francisco de Peralta, an open, candid type, went to jail on the night of the crime rather than testify, leaving the historian to surmise that Cetina, more dead than alive, had whispered from his bed: "Say nothing." Peralta, shocked and fretting about who was to take care of Cetina, as he himself said, was too angry and upset "to have any memory or to say anything coherent."[40] Not badly wounded himself, and after a night in jail had restored his memory, he at last gave rein to his natural candor and forthrightness. So, the *alcalde* went to the jail the next day and found him quieter and more tranquil in spirit, despite the indignity and "injury of prison," and quite willing to testify. After a recitation almost as graphic as that the poet himself gave three weeks later, he openly replied when asked if he knew his assailants that he suspected Hernando de Nava was one of them. Hernando was not only known to be in town, but, for no cause at all, bore him ill will because he jealously suspected that this witness courted the same woman of

39 Not one scintilla of awareness that Cetina wrote verse appears in this long, prolix process. This ignorance, however, was natural enough; the public in Spain did not recognize him as a poet either. See p. 83, n. 84.

40 "Con alteración e no tiene memoria. . . ." AGI, México, 95, fs. 4v.–5. Nearly three weeks later he told Judge-Investigator Martínez he could not then testify "por estar como estava muy alterado e enojado y parecerle que no se podia reportar para dezir cosa concertada conforme a lo que avia pasado." *Ibid.*, f. 45v.

whom it was bruited about in the city that "the said Nava had communication." Not even he involved Madame de la Torre.

Though an assumption of a woman problem runs beneath all the questioning, the sole disrespectful reference to Doña Leonor gets into the record from the mouth of a twelve-year-old Nava slave testifying under torture. In jail, stroking his beard reflectively, Hernando had confided to his friends within earshot of this his waiting boy that he would make that good-for-nothing, "that whore," Leonor de Osma, pay for jilting him and for good measure "throw out the whole kit and caboodle."[41] The other servants were open to trivial questions on points of known fact, but they gave no hint of any liaison, triangle, or quadrangle such as this one appears to have been. Long after Nava came under suspicion, the slave woman Yseo readily acknowledged that Nava had walked and did walk, sometimes afoot and sometimes mounted, by the house of her master,[42] but, as she knew, so had hundreds of others.

Scene Two
"Thou Swindling Traitor"

In this state of affairs, on May 2, thirty-one days after the assault upon Cetina, "along toward one o'clock, just about when matins sounded,"[43] a whispering voice that Doña Leonor quietly and even tenderly recognized called her (*quedito*) to the window while her husband, "Dotor"

41 See Appendix III.
42 AGI, México, 95, f. 79v. Confesión de Yseo, negra, Ciudad de los Angeles, 21 de abril de 1554.
43 *Ibid.*, f. 121. Confesión de Yseo, negra, Ciudad de los Angeles, 3 de mayo de 1554.

de la Torre, slumbered in his warm place—a weakness altogether unsuitable to a cuckold. Her version, though, was that while asking "Who's there?" she unsuspectingly thrust her nose to the iron grill covering a window that gave onto a small corridor within the house, and a dagger slashed down across her nose and face. "Take that," said the tender voice, "to remember me by and call your husband here so I can kill him."

Bloody and horrified, surely, she made her way back to her bed and, no longer solicitous of her husband's rest, cried out to him that Hernando de Nava was there and that he had wounded her in the face. So precipitately did the doctor arise that, still in his night shirt, he looked in vain for his sword. Settling for a lance, which he grasped with the grace of Don Quixote, and shouting, "Negroes! Negroes!" he sallied out into the corridor, yelling "Hernando de Nava, thou swindling traitor!"—plain indication that the doctor now at last recognized that his house was betrayed. When he discovered that young Galeote was there seconding Nava, he went into the plural: "You swindling traitors! What do you want in the middle of the night—to murder my Negroes?"[44]

While De la Torre thus gave vent to his astonishment and outrage, Nava was climbing from the flat roof of the low corridor to the main roof, his route of escape. At this point, Juan Galán, a Negro slave, took up the sword his master was too nervous to locate and pursued the intruder. Nava, seeing what was happening, warned: "You come closer, nigger, and I'll kill you." Galán, a man's man, advanced anyway and, instead of thrusting the swinging man in the back as he deserved, deliberately took him by

44 *Ibid.*, fs. 117–19v. Confesión de Leonor de Osma, 3 de mayo de 1554.

the foot to prevent his escaping over the roof. Nava let go and, drawing his sword, attacked Galán, who, calm as a finished fencer, expertly parried every thrust. Then, when Nava shouted "Kill him!" Galán wheeled just in time to see Galeote slash him in the sword arm from behind. His weapon then fell, and in the fury of the assault upon him Galán fell over after it, but, accurately measuring his helplessness and his danger, he fled the scene.[45] Cecilia, a Negress, apparently Juan Galán's woman, ventured to pass Nava on this flat roof of the interior corridor only to get a bloody wound in her thigh from this woman-fighting son of a Conqueror.[46] Yseo, a black slave woman, then took the keys, opened the street door, and began to cry up the neighborhood.[47] At that juncture Nava and Galeote, seeing and hearing that the street door was open, ran toward it. De la Torre, now a bit bolder, looked out his window in time to see a man he took to be Martín de Mafra, brother of Gonzalo Galeote, enter the house and shout to his confederates inside that the door was open. When these two then ran out through it, instead of scurrying off, they turned about to menace the doctor and to tell him "with ugly words" that they would kill him if he came out into the street. Then, slowly and calmly, they filed off toward the Dominican monastery where they were "fortified."

Inside the house with the candles at last lighted, the servants assembled to see their mistress bleeding from a gash across her nose, Juan Galán with so much blood

---

45 *Ibid.*, fs. 222v.–23v. Confesión de Juan Galán, negro del dotor de la Torre, Los Angeles, 3 de febrero de 1554.

46 *Ibid.*, fs. 252–53v. Confesión de Cecilia, negra, Ciudad de los Angeles, 10 de mayo de 1554.

47 *Ibid.*, fs. 121–22. Confesión de Yseo, negra, Ciudad de los Angeles, 3 de mayo de 1554.

pouring from his arm that he thought he would lose it, and Cecilia bleeding so from her thigh wound that she had shouted, "They have killed me!"[48] Leonor Ramírez, De la Torre's grandmother-in-law, now had time to regret that when she heard Nava open the window, she thought it was just some cats,[49] as, naturally, it was time for them rather than men to be aprowl. Turning from this uproar, De la Torre hastened to the house of the judge-investigator who, with his notary and constable filed back to the De la Torre house to witness this woebegone scene.[50] In a happier moment, he might have reflected how in three years, surrounded with a new set of slaves, he had come again into prosperity—and into danger.

The attack upon the De la Torre household on Wednesday, May 2, by young, high-placed scoundrels, sallying from ecclesiastical sanctuary and retreating there at their pleasure for a full month after the assault on Gutierre de Cetina, raised the pitch of official anxiety a full octave. Judge-Investigator Martínez, calling witnesses and taking depositions for four weeks, had actually encountered Gonzalo Galeote on horseback only to look impotently on as the fugitive gave his horse full rein and beat the judge —if, indeed, his honor accepted the indignity of a race— to sanctuary in the Dominican convent. Now with this second scandal and with the accused not even behind bars, he had more than the gauntlet laid down to him; he had his honor and reputation at stake. The people were now actually flocking to the Dominican convent, much as

---

48 *Ibid.*, f. 121v. Confesión de Yseo, negra, Ciudad de los Angeles, 3 de mayo de 1554.

49 *Ibid.*, f. 119v. Confesión de Leonor Ramírez, aguela [*sic*] de la dicha Leonor de Osma, Ciudad de los Angeles, 3 de mayo de 1554.

50 *Ibid.*, fs. 241–43v. Dr. Pedro de la Torre: su confesión, Ciudad de los Angeles, 10 de mayo de 1554.

people might run to a great fire, and were in fact already crowding in when he left the De la Torre house.

He now abandoned his measured, judicial pace for peremptory methods. On Thursday, the day after this latest crime, he ordered the ecclesiastical judge (*provisor*) to deliver up these swordsmen on the ground that they had forfeited sanctuary—left the protection of the church—when they committed these outrages. The churchmen adamantly refused, imposed an interdict, and excommunicated the judge-investigator. On Friday, May 4, as the judge forged on, the *provisor*, the Dominican prior and friars, with some Franciscans and Augustinians, the archdeacon and other priests, formed a procession behind a cross covered with black mourning (*luto negro*), went to the main altar (*altar mayor*), took a monstrance they said contained the holy sacrament, filed out chanting "In exitu Israel de Aegypto," and would not consent that a solitary person accompany the sacrament as "they were all excommunicated." The very words they chose to sing —Psalm 114—made this defiance of Judge Martínez greater than nature itself. "When Israel came out of Egypt . . ." with Judah as "his sanctuary," even as they came out of the monastery, "the sea . . . fled; Jordan was driven back. The mountains skipped like young rams, and the little hills like young sheep. . . . Tremble thou earth. . . ." To these friars and clerics this was earth-shaking business.[51]

Certain that his prey had taken refuge in the tower of the monastery, Judge Martínez immediately ordered harquebusiers and archers to give covering fire while others there threw up ladders to take the tower from above and

51 *Ibid.*, fs. 128v.–30v., 137–38. Proceso contra Hernando de Nava, Ciudad de los Angeles, 4 de mayo de 1554.

—a note of modernity—had straw and pepper burned to smoke out the tower, which, with luck, they did not smoke to the ground.[52] The quarry, though, did not reason as expected. That night—Friday, May 4—Gonzalo Galeote let himself down a rope thrown out a window, jumped into the fig orchard, and fled the city.[53]

To the friars, now step-by-step cast in the role of *particeps criminis,* this news was most welcome, for Hernando de Nava had disappeared at the same time. The next morning Frey Luis de San Miguel, friar-presbyter of the Augustinian order, came to the monastery and went before the judge-investigator, who must have felt a little less than glee at the news, to swear that Nava and Galeote "had let themselves down ropes from the tower before midnight and flown the monastery." Judge Martínez, at the same time, said he wanted to open the door of the tower then locked and barricaded. When Fray Tomás de San Juan, prior of the monastery, arrived at this juncture he said "he thanked Our Lord that the fugitives had gone from the monastery." Exuberant, he gave the judge-investigator permission to open the tower and see for himself.[54]

---

52 The reader should know that this man is the judge-investigator, or special judge (*juez pesquisidor*) Bachelor Alonso Martínez, and that this action, taking place on Friday, May 4, 1554, came the very day Luis de Velasco and the judges of the royal *audiencia* in Mexico City appointed one of their number, Dr. Antonio Mejía, to go to Puebla de los Angeles and bring under control a crime, compounded by conspiracy, that was already out of hand. Martínez, alarmed by the brutal assault on Leonor de Osma on Wednesday night, had at last resorted to force on Friday. When Mejía arrived on Saturday, he had no need, despite what some have asserted (for example, Francisco Rodríguez Marín in Menéndez y Pelayo, *Historia de la poesía,* I, 29, n. 1) to use force.

53 AGI, México, 95, fs. 166–73. Confesión de Hernando de Nava, 12 de mayo de 1554.

54 *Ibid.,* f. 145. De como salieron los delincuentes de la torre donde estaban retraydos por vnos cordeles dexado los grillos.

Scene Three
The Wages of "Crime upon Crime"

Back in Mexico City, thirty-six hours after Nava slashed Leonor de Osma, the alarmed royal *audiencia* reacted vigorously and decisively. That Nava and Galeote had taken sanctuary and "with little fear of God and contempt for royal justice" went on piling crime upon crime with the help of townspeople was a threat to the crown and an intolerable outrage besides.[55] Because of the gravity of the crime, Viceroy Luis de Velasco and the *oidores* felt that a person of quality—some high official—whose prestige was commensurate with the task in Puebla de los Angeles should replace Bachelor Martínez. They accordingly appointed the *oidor* Antonio Mejía on May 4, the day Galeote escaped, and gave him sweeping authority "to seize the bodies, sequester the property, hear the parties . . . and sentence and punish as justice requires."[56] The

55 As an indication of the size of these interrelated families and the danger of conspiracy between them, Gonzalo Galeote's father testified that, when he had been married seventeen years, he had a pregnant wife, six sons, and five daughters, "some of them marriageable." Hernando de Nava, whose father died seventeen years after coming out with Pánfilo de Narváez in 1520, swore that his father left seven sons (children?). (Icaza [ed.], *Conquistadores y pobladores*, I, 80–81, II, 15–16.) The record of his trial, AGI, México, 95, f. 240, shows that there were at least two daughters. As the mother remarried, there must have been half brothers also.

56 AGI, México, 95, fs. 148v.–52v. Otra comisión que el virrey y la audiencia le dió al dotor Mexia . . . , México, 4 de mayo de 1554. The succession of investigators and judges, each more important than the last, reflects the ever-rising concern of the viceregal authorities over the case. Considering that Mexico City was eighty-one miles from Puebla (Ciudad de los Angeles), the viceroy and *audiencia* adapted themselves to the changing circumstances of the distant case with remarkable expedition. Thus, the *alcalde*, Pedro Moreno, near midnight on April 1, 1554, as was legal and customary, began to take

next day, Saturday, when Dr. Mejía reached Puebla de los Angeles[57] with orders to take over the papers Martínez had accumulated and proceed with the case, he was greeted, as he was bound to be, with the news that the prisoners had escaped.

Mejía now moved with the same celerity that had brought him the eighty-one miles from Mexico City from one day to the next. He could plainly see the deteriorated situation the royal *audiencia* had assigned him to correct. His predecessor had violated the Dominican sanctuary and lighted a fire of straw and pepper in the tower. Priests and friars of all ranks were in a hubbub, openly siding with the Nava faction and tendering it concrete help. Within six days he had sentenced the chief malefactor.

Before noon on his first full day, with the judge-investigator Martínez, a retinue of justices of all kinds, and with

---

evidence, which he continued to do until April 9 (fs. 12–24), but he lacked the power, if not the authority, to control the band of Nava partisans, now grown lawless. The wanton attack upon Cetina and Peralta, followed as it was by a quick jailbreak, with the culprits holed up in the Dominican monastery, sallying forth at night in friar's garb and with tonsured heads, duly brought in on April 9 Martín de Calahorra, lieutenant *corregidor*, delegate of the most powerful royal official in the district. On his first day, Calahorra actually heard the poet's first declaration (fs. 24–25). However, the viceroy and *audiencia* in Mexico City, on April 13 when Calahorra had been at work only four days, appointed Bachelor Alonso Martínez as judge-investigator (*juez pesquisidor*) and sent him on April 16 to investigate and punish the guilty. Three days later, when Cetina had regained enough strength, Martínez heard the graphic unfolding of the assault upon him and his companion from the poet's own lips (fs. 30–33), one month after a fever had detained him in the city. With the attack upon the wife of Dr. de la Torre, however, the royal *audiencia* turned on May 4 (fs. 148v.–52v.) to a man of still greater prestige, Dr. Antonio Mejía, a member of the royal *audiencia* itself, as special judge (*juez de comisión*). He arrived the next day—surely after traveling all night.

57 *Ibid.*, fs. 154–55v.

the idle running along and frisking around them, he made his way to the Dominican convent. There he ran into a veritable clamor of informants. If Nava and Galeote "had ever been there," he heard on every side, "they still were." Mejía thereupon had his men send for other searchers and ordered them to search and ransack every room, passage, and cranny from top to bottom of the monastery so that, if the criminals were not there, he could raise the cordon thrown around the building. He ordered the searchers, in case they found either refugee, to put him under guard and proceed. As the Dominicans now believed, or at least professed to believe, that the fugitives had escaped, and felt unmenaced by any threat or use of force, they freely opened their doors.

With these friars around him, Judge Mejía, with calm and dignity and in company with Bachelor Martínez, "walked along in the said monastery searching the upstairs and downstairs rooms [*piezas*] without forcing open or breaking down any doors or walls, and bringing friars along" with those doing the searching,[58] until at last he heard voices from a certain quarter. Hastening there, his lordship found that Alguacil Pedro de Flores had come upon Nava. It was, consequently, not only an olfactory but a legal embarrassment when, on this Sunday morning, they pulled the slinking Nava ignominiously down "from a plank over the necessaries" in a fetor so foul that previous searchers had bobbed back out too soon. Hernando de Nava had had no stomach for Galeote's derring-do on ropes! There was, in his language, "no suitable conjuncture" for it.[59]

So, after cheerfully accompanying the judge, the friars,

58 *Ibid.*, f. 162–62v.
59 *Ibid.*, fs. 166v–73.

patently chagrined at his success, would then detain him for the violence done. As Martínez filed off to the jail with the prisoner, Mejía, instead of bursting with anger at this attempt to confine a judge of the royal *audiencia*, calmly sat down, saying, "Very well, I will hear you out." When he had done so, he asked them to put their particulars in writing, arose, and took his departure. Immediately thereafter, he joined Martínez at the jail and formally assumed jurisdiction over the inquiry.

Nava's defense was logical but thin. Indeed, to hear him tell it, his communion with everyone was like unto that of the saints; he had no anger against anybody and no suspicion against any man on account of mortal woman.[60] His story had it that he was not "over twenty-five," as he gave it when first arrested,[61] but only twenty-three, as he stated three weeks later[62] when he had had time to get legal advice. Being under twenty-five, then, enabled a man to use his minority as an extenuating circumstance. Besides, Nava's position was that he had not gone out the night Cetina was ambushed, and as he was confined under sanctuary in the Dominican convent at the time, it was not possible he could have gashed Madame de la Torre.

Mejía countered these yarns and cut them to shreds with a new parade of old witnesses, some called back to testify on these new points, and others—all critically placed blacks—to tell a new story under threat of torture. Everybody in the De la Torre household, as he knew they

---

60 *Ibid.*, f. 167. Confesión de Hernando de Nava, Ciudad de los Angeles, 6 de mayo de 1554.
61 *Ibid.*, f. 6v. Confesión de Hernando de Nava, Ciudad de los Angeles, 1 de abril de 1554.
62 *Ibid.*, f. 164–64v. Confesión de Hernando de Nava, Ciudad de los Angeles, 6 de mayo de 1554.

would, testified that Nava was the man, that they knew him well, both by sight and by voice. One of them, the Negress María, testified not only that she knew him well, but that she knew his voice and heard him talk.[63] Mejía even called De la Torre himself to testify to Nava's perfidies, though there was always danger, as De la Torre's careful skirting of motives indicates, that the doctor's honor was tottering.

The accumulated evidence, though Judge Martínez had begun another round of "declarations" the day after the attack on Leonor de Osma, had not penetrated officially what every man thought he knew privately. This Mejía was determined to do, come what would of the honor of gentlemen and the terror of servants. In such a sweep, his inquiry embraced both the Cetina and the De la Torre cases. On May 10 he got an extended *confesión* from Dr. de la Torre that contained much militating against Nava and Galeote, but produced little that would pass the review of the *audiencia* back in Mexico City.[64]

The next day, then, Judge Mejía showed that he was tired of the tight lips among the slaves. He found no fault with the honor of Cetina or, for that matter, of De la Torre that would let them name no woman, though Cetina should lose his life and De la Torre his pride. At the jail he called Francisco, a twelve-year-old Negro slave

---

63 *Ibid.*, fs. 248–53v. Confesiones de Leonor de Osma, Leonor Ramírez, Yseo, María, y Juan Galán, Ciudad de los Angeles, 10 de mayo de 1554.

64 On the other hand, Lázaro de la Roca, who had harbored Leonor de Osma de la Torre in her trysts with Francisco de Peralta, testified plainly that Hernando de Nava, while enjoying sanctuary in the Dominican choir, had said that "they say your worship deserved the slash that Cetina got. . . ." *Ibid.*, f. 163. Confesión de Lázaro de la Roca, Ciudad de los Angeles, 10 de mayo de 1554. Icaza, *Sucesos reales*, 238.

"Question of Torture"
Courtesy Archivo General de Indias, Audiencia de México, Legajo 95, f. 285

and waiting boy to young Hernando in the Nava household, who denied that he knew anything more than he had told in his previous testimony when he had said he did not go out of the house on the night of the assault on Cetina. The judge interrupted to say that, in view of the importance of the case and the closeness of this boy to Nava, he would authorize putting the "question of torture." Even among slaves, where chivalry did not flower as it did with the poet, this torture astride a donkey was never comic. Mounted facing the hind end, with his hands tied and his feet corded together under the lowly beast, his companions standing around him with their eyes apop, the meanest man could hardly fail to feel shame; he was too horrified to feel anger. With a tourniquet around the victim's arm, a constable stood by to give the stick as many twists as necessary to produce satisfactory speech—as they invariably and immediately did.

Francisco required only the preliminary two turns to discover a new fount of information. He then gushed forth with incisive evidence that, in its quick fluency and striking verisimilitude, neatly rounded out what was known of the attack upon Cetina, Nava's quick break from jail, and his disfiguring of Leonor de Osma. As Nava's body servant and his boy-spy, he was an eyewitness in all three episodes.[65] With such testimony admissible, the judge could prove that the premeditated attack from ambush was made upon both Cetina and Peralta—not just upon Peralta and accidentally upon Cetina. The curiously fluent little slave brought the wife of De la Torre out into the open as the motive for the rampage now beginning, explained the conspiracy that got Nava

---

65 AGI, México, 95, fs. 284–92v. Confesión de Francisco, negro esclavo, Ciudad de los Angeles, 11 de mayo de 1554.

Francisco, Negro Slave, Describes Attack upon Cetina
Courtesy Archivo General de Indias, Audiencia de México, Legajo 95, f. 286v.

out of jail the night after the attack on Cetina, implicitly exonerated the Franciscans of participation in that feat, implicated a dozen other individuals by name, and, when he came to the De la Torre house, gave testimony that dovetailed to a nicety with that already given by witnesses from there.

His explicit evidence on what happened "the night they wounded Cetina" both confirmed and elaborated what the poet himself had said. Francisco heard Hernando de Nava, Gonzalo Galeote, Pedro Páez, and Martín de Mafra talking on the street about "whether they should go and kill the said Gutierre de Cetina and Francisco de Peralta," when Martín de Mafra burst out: "I swear to God I've got to kill them; they've followed me three or four nights." That night, after dining with Bishop Martín de Hojacastro at the house of Juan Sarmiento, Nava, Galeote, Páez, and Mafra, their conspiracy settled, stopped at the corral of Hernando de Villanueva, across the street from Dr. de la Torre's. Pedro Páez took the buckler from Francisco and Nava took the casque.[66] The little Negro they then sent forward to warn of anyone's coming. When he knew that Cetina and Peralta were coming, "because they came playing," he quickly notified Nava who, with his companions, posted himself at the corner of the corral. Whispering, "Don't come any farther; wait for me here; I'm going ahead and let them have it," Nava jumped out, his two-handed broadsword (*montante*) unsheathed, and gave Cetina a slash across the face that felled him like a beef. Thereupon, me-too Galeote gave him a cut in the head, also with the monstrous *montante*.

With Cetina prostrate, the attackers "took out" after Peralta, "who was running away," and, joined now by

66 *Ibid.*, f. 286.

Martín de Mafra, gave him many blows as he lay on the ground instinctively parrying them. Then—one imagines him placing his sword point down—Nava said: "If I wanted to kill you, I very well could." From this scene, they went toward the Dominican monastery and then back to Juan Sarmiento's. Here again, Nava posted Francisco and ordered him "to watch out that nobody appears." Páez and Martín de Mafra left the house, while Galeote and Martín de Soseguera, who had never left it, stayed on with Hernando de Nava, who ordered his waiting boy to make his bed. Then, with what must have been habitual dominance, he turned to Galeote and said: "Your worship, go and see how Cetina is." Presently he came back to report that they had already sent for somebody to treat him.[67]

On the second day after his arrest, Nava, though wearing shackles with an iron ball, had slipped away from jail, thus adding another mystery to the case that Francisco could clear up. For thirty-nine days the town was full of rumor and speculation about the mysterious jailbreak. The details of the escape, however, were known to so many people that wide hostility to the civil authority, especially on the part of the Nava family and the religious and ecclesiastical authorities, must be assumed. Francisco, still sitting in a state of suspended terror on the burro, spouted out the names of some dozen relatives and cronies who, on different occasions, had conspired to bring off Nava's escape.[68]

---

67 *Ibid.*, f. 287.
68 These men were Juan Sarmiento, Hernando de Villanueva, San Juan de Zúñiga (brother-in-law), Martín de Soseguera, Diego de Hojeda, Francisco de Reynoso, Diego de Villanueva, Juan de Cisneros, "a mestizo," [Fulano] Carvallar Mansilla, Gonzalo Galeote, and Martín de Mafra.

75

Unfortunately for the jailer, after securing his prisoner with ball and chain and locking him in his cell, he allowed Francisco to bring food and friends to dine with the confined man. When these, conspiring in Juan Sarmiento's house, had their plans ready, Hernando de Villanueva came to the jail and in the presence of Francisco said to Nava: "Listen, don't fool us; we are going to spring you tonight." Besides, San Juan de Zúñiga had assured the prisoner: "We are more than ready." At suppertime on the second evening, Hernando de Villanueva and Martín de Soseguera, who had been delegated to provide the ropes, went into the jail to join Nava in the supper Francisco had brought. Villanueva, as was hardly strange, ate one mouthful only.

Every man in the conspiracy except Juan Sarmiento, who stayed at home, shared in what now took place. Gonzalo Galeote, Juan de Cisneros, "the mestizo," and Carvallar Mansilla (Mançanilla)[69] went up on the roof, and Martín de Mafra, Francisco de Reynoso, Diego de Hojeda, and San Juan de Zúñiga stayed below to keep watch on the lane. After Jailer Flores came in, Nava engaged him in conversation apart,[70] while Soseguera bade all a casual adieu and went to join his comrades in the lane at the back of the jail. Then Hernando de Villanueva went toward the main door with the jailer, talking, only to leave the door to Nava's cell open. Nava, who had managed to remove the drawbolt on his shackles the night before, lifted up the great ball on the chain and said that if anybody came for him, "he had only to smite him with this"

69 This man is the only one whose first name Francisco did not know exactly.
70 This circumstance, plus the too-easy removal of the drawbolt, suggests the involvement of the jailer.

76

and take off the fetters. When the jailer opened the door to the street for Hernando de Villanueva, Nava went to the patio, and those on the roof threw him a rope and pulled him up as the Indians began to shout that Nava had escaped. The young men then let themselves down in a hurry, as planned, into the back lane where others were on guard, pulled in the ropes, and all ran off, "each to his own taste." The taste of Nava, Mafra, and Galeote was for taking sanctuary in the church of the Dominican monastery. Mafra's running for asylum when not yet accused is evidence that he considered himself guilty—along with Nava and Galeote—in the sneaking and merciless assault upon Cetina and Peralta.

What a contradiction in jailing methods! Coming and going in the jail was on the same order as visits between the salons of aristocrats and was undertaken with the same courtly, measured deliberation. The prisoner himself, though, bore not just the name Hernando, as was natural for the son of one of Hernando Cortés' men, but also bore a set of shackles fit to restrain a giant and correspondingly uncomfortable. The young slave's story ended, or should have ended, all speculation on this puzzling escape. How much it indicates that, given a little exposure to hardship, these men might have conquered a race, as did their fathers!

Francisco, pausing only to give his intermittent explanation for not speaking up in his previous testimony, rushed headlong into the De la Torre aspect of the case. Thus, on Wednesday, the vespers of Ascension, May 2, 1554, when Hernando de Nava, Gonzalo Galeote, and Martín de Mafra were *retraydos* in the Dominican monastery, Francisco went there to take his master's food and overheard the three as they "concerted to go out that night and knife the wife of Dr. de la Torre." Once again they pulled Francisco in as a spy to keep an eye out for people passing. Then as they were creeping along the wall of the corral from the monastery toward Dr. de la Torre's, a man came along, and Nava ducked down to avoid being seen. Once by Dr. de la Torre's house, Nava and Galeote left Mafra to keep watch at the corner, then climbed up over the grill of a window on an adjoining house, and pulled the little Negro Francisco up after them. Him they pushed ahead into the house to see that none of the Negroes were moving about. Finding the house quiet, he so told his master who, separating from Galeote, went along a stairway to a window with a grill and gave a signal. Then, "the doctor's wife came out, half opened the window, and asked, 'Who's there, a Negro?' " Now followed the melee in which Leonor de Osma was cut across the face, Juan Galán slashed with a broadsword in the right arm, and Cecilia given a vicious stab in the thigh.

All these incidents, except the stabbing of Cecilia, are more particularly described by members of the De la Torre household—the only aspect of all three of these crises in which Francisco is not more specific and convincing than anybody else. Francisco, however, does confirm Dr. de la Torre's testimony that Martín de Mafra was waiting outside as Galeote and Nava ran out. That Francisco was in the house all that time and ran out with the others without being noticed by anybody, particularly by Dr. de la Torre, seems strange, though there must have been a great commotion of Negroes in the house and, it goes without saying, Francisco made himself inconspicuous in the hubbub. After walking around for a while, the three criminals, Francisco with them, went to the main door of the convent, a friar let them in, and they went to bed.

In what Francisco said there is direct testimony that Yseo, Leonor de Osma's maid, came and went between Nava and her mistress with letters and that Leonor also came and went to talk with Nava at the cart-yard door at the back of the monastery. How Yseo answered questions patently based on this evidence will soon appear.

With this last bit, the judge from Mexico City ordered Francisco down from the burro and had him untied, but not before he had given him an opportunity to explain why he had lied in the first place by saying he had not gone out of the house the night of the attack on Cetina. He had reason enough, and he related it graphically. Juan Sarmiento, a protector of Nava, perhaps a relative, always in the background, and San Juan de Zúñiga, Nava's brother-in-law, had menaced him, promising to scald him with hot grease[71] and to kill him if he breathed a word. Meanwhile, Nava reinforced these threats with many "boxes and blows."[72] In fact, he actually did scald and burn Francisco over his whole body and, especially on the buttocks, "which he had very burned." At the end of this pitiful testimony, the judge ordered an examination and found many sores, marks, scars, and burns. To this result of the examination, the judge duly required witnesses to affix their signatures.[73]

All the internal evidence indicates that Francisco in straightforward and truthful testimony was imprecise

71 *Pringar,* the equivalent of "to tar" with hot tar and a standing punishment for criminal or recalcitrant slaves.
72 With "muchos moxicones y golpes. . . ."
73 AGI, México, 95, fs. 284–92. Confesión de Francisco, negro esclavo, Ciudad de los Angeles, 11 de mayo de 1554.

only where he was not an eyewitness. He testified that Martín de Mafra, Galeote's brother, stood guard in both the assault on Cetina and upon Leonor de Osma. Francisco de Peralta, who, unlike Cetina, never lost consciousness, saw two or three forms—just enough latitude to allow for Mafra. Dr. de la Torre bore out the boy's word when he declared that a man he took to be Martín de Mafra was on guard outside his house during Nava's and Galeote's invasion of it, though he did not suspect, in the movement of his household, that a slave of Nava's was among his own Negroes. Francisco's testimony that Nava and Galeote took him along to keep an eye out for people and to carry a shield and casque has too fine a ring of authenticity to be ignored. He warned of the approach of Cetina and Peralta and knew it was they because they came playing, as Cetina himself swore. He alone touches the strongest probability when he claimed that Peralta was running away when overtaken or, perhaps, intercepted and pounded on the ground. He claimed that Nava, back at the house of his host after the attack on the poet, sent Galeote to see how Cetina was and, nicely dovetailing, De la Torre swore that Galeote did approach him with this precise inquiry.

Francisco's description of Nava's escape from jail the night after his attack upon Cetina is too detailed, too complicated, and too incriminating for a boy of twelve to have invented while sitting backwards on a burro before an *oidor* of the royal *audiencia*. Other niceties strongly indicating a straightforward eyewitness account are that when approaching for the attack upon the De la Torre household, Nava, when he saw a man coming, ducked down so that he would not be recognized; that when

Leonor de Osma answered the whispered call at her window, she only half opened it while she asked: "Who's there, a Negro?"[74] Such caution is highly indicated at such a moment.

Now, after this testimony, was the time to call the Negress Yseo, whom Francisco implicated in her mistress' amours. This confidential maid of Madame de la Torre, mounted on a donkey and tied in the same humiliating way as was Francisco, likewise required only certain twists of the tourniquet to say that she would talk. And talk she did. Hernando had gone many times, day and night, to the house of her mistress. There, among other things, he had repeatedly quarreled with her because she frequented the house of Lázaro de la Roca, next to the house where lived Francisco de Peralta, of whom Nava was jealous. He even ordered her not to go anywhere[75] without his permission. Yseo noticed that when her master commanded Doña Leonor "to go out to take her pleasure, she did not dare for the fear she had of Hernando de Nava. . . ."

She denied she had ever carried letters between her mistress and Nava—a flat contradiction of the testimony of the Negro boy Francisco[76]—but Yseo was mature enough at twenty-five[77] and, as the personal maid of a shameless woman, experienced enough to know that hedging was possible even under torture. She did admit, though, that her mistress had gone into the church of Santo Domingo by the back door when Nava was fortified

74 That is, a servant.
75 "Ni fuese a ningun cabo. . . ."
76 AGI, México, 95, f. 291v.
77 *Ibid.*, f. 179v. Confesión de Yseo, Ciudad de los Angeles, 21 de abril de 1554.

processes so fast, though these were always faster-paced than civil suits. Besides, in capital cases there was no appeal over the royal *audiencia*—already horrified enough to send one of its members off on a race to Puebla. Be that as it may, on May 12 the judge, Dr. Mejía, gave Nava as stiff a sentence as any man ever got whose mother had fifty thousand ducats and as much influence as there was in the Indies.[85]

First, Nava, a rope around his neck, mounted on a beast of burden, tied hand and foot, the town crier going ahead preconizing the event, would ride through "the public and customary" streets to the one that Dr. de la Torre lived on. There his right hand would be cut off and raised on a pole. From there, on the same animal, he would ride to the public plaza of the city where the public executioner would behead him. The sentence also called for the confiscation of the arms with which Nava was taken and for the costs of the action. Dr. Mejía's unmerciful sentence reflected horror at Nava's wanton conduct and, no doubt, irritation at the ecclesiastical intervention.[86]

Nava's guardian immediately appealed to the royal *audiencia* in Mexico City with the plain intention of appealing as many times as he legally could.[87] Mejía neither responded to nor executed this appeal. The guardian, through his lawyer in Puebla, then wrote directly to Judge Mejía with the plea that he accept appeal on the ground that his ward (*"mi menor"*) had not been given

85 AGI, México, 95, fs. 326v.–27. Sentencia del juez de comisión, Ciudad de los Angeles, 12 de mayo de 1554.
86 See p. 87, n. 97.
87 AGI, México, 95, fs. 327–28v. Apelación de Hernando de Nava, Ciudad de los Angeles, 12 de mayo de 1554.

enough time to present all the evidence in his favor.[88] Instead, the judge ordered Nava taken up to Mexico City in chains and irons under a formidable escort.[89] This decisive step removed the danger of a second rescue of Nava from the jail in Puebla. Moreover, as Nava's lawyer in Mexico City handled his appeals to the royal *audiencia*, keeping the prisoner in Puebla could only mean delay.

In the capital, the lawyer, Juan Ruiz de Rojas, in his appeal to the *audiencia*, pretended that Hernando de Nava, now in the viceregal or court jail in Mexico City, could not have been guilty of the bloody slashings in the De la Torre house as "he spent the entire night closed up in the said monastery." Moreover, Ruiz insisted, his client had not been allowed the legal time limits for the presentation of his case.[90] The *oidores* accepted the appeal and ordered more than once that the files of papers in the action be supplied complete to Nava's lawyer.[91] Even so, Juan Ruiz kept asking in vain for the file.[92] The case, nevertheless, was ready for the *audiencia* to present to its fiscal on June 14. The tide now turned against Nava. The fiscal found Dr. Antonio Mejía's sentence just and recommended to the royal *audiencia* that it execute the sentence on the person of Hernando de Nava.[93] That body now

88 *Ibid.*, fs. 342v.–43v. El licenciado Antonio Caballero al Dr. Mejía. Ciudad de los Angeles, 17 de mayo de 1554.
89 *Ibid.*, f. 344v. Auto del doctor Antonio Mejía, oidor de la real audiencia, Ciudad de los Angeles, 18 de mayo de 1554.
90 *Ibid.*, fs. 369–69v., 370–70v. Juan Ruiz de Rojas a la Real Audiencia, México, s. f.
91 See for example, *ibid.*, f. 374v. Auto de la real audiencia, México, 27 de junio de 1554.
92 *Ibid.*, f. 373v. Juan Ruiz de Rojas a la real audiencia, México, s. f., 1554.
93 *Ibid.*, f. 374–74v. Dictamen del fiscal, México, s. f.

formally began its review, but, as if exasperated with the defense, suddenly broke off all further appeal and ordered that, since Judge Mejía had "condemned the said Hernando de Nava to have his right hand cut off," that sentence be immediately carried out in Mexico City.[94]

That same day, two months and one week after the assault on Cetina, the high constable (*alguacil mayor*) in Mexico City, who now took custody of the prisoner, carried out Nava's new sentence in the great plaza. Thither the constable escorted the young man through the streets, on a beast of burden, preceded by the public crier. Then Dr. Torres, physician and surgeon,[95] in the presence of Viceroy Luis de Velasco and the members of the royal *audiencia*, cut off Nava's right hand. With this gruesome relic nailed up in the place customary in such cases, the crier defied anybody, on pain of death, to take it away. For his part, Nava waited, unimpressed and unaware that he had just enjoyed the honor of having this useful member detached by the first man ever to be examined for the degree of doctor of medicine from a university in the Western Hemisphere.[96] At last, everything certified with

94 *Ibid.*, f. 375–75v. Auto de vista de la audiencia de México, 7 de julio de 1554.

95 Damián de Torres had been examined the year before in the newly inaugurated Royal and Pontifical University of Mexico by a committee of men, some of whom had no medical training or degrees, and on December 1, also in the presence of Luis de Velasco, awarded the degree of doctor of medicine. Cristóbal Bernardo de la Plaza y Jaén, *Crónica de la Real y Pontificia Universidad de México*, ed. Nicolás Rangel (2 vols.; México, 1931), I, 37.

96 Plaza y Jaén, *Crónica*, I, 46, says that on August 10, 1553, the Royal and Pontifical University of México "incorporated" Dr. Juan de Alcázar's degree of doctor of medicine from the University of Lérida. Though Dr. Alcázar is presented in the index (*Ibid.*, II, 334) as "el primero que se graduó en la facultad de medicina," the cloister min-

the utmost scrupulosity, the high constable conducted the prisoner back to jail,[97] from which he never emerged, for all this process tells—all 776 pages of it. Nothing was said, and nothing more is ever said, in all this voluminous record of the beheading imposed by Judge Mejía. Nava had survived.

A death sentence, though, is too much to get lost by casual oversight. Least of all does such a loss accord with the Spanish genius for recording legal detail. The same record that cavalierly passes—so it seems on the surface —over the little matter of not executing the death sentence scrupulously orders that a copy of the lawyer's petition for the armor and arms taken from Nava be given to the fiscal.[98] Moreover, Judge Mejía followed up the grim mutilation in Mexico City with orders that the Indians in Hernando de Nava's *encomienda* of Castilblanco pay their tributes to Catalina Vélez, Nava's mother, to cover

---

utes show that the University of Mexico merely validated his doctor's degree. (AGN, Universidad, II, f. 86, Claustro de 10 de agosto de 1553.) A case could also be made—and sometimes is—on behalf of another as the first man to receive the degree of doctor of medicine in the same university. When Pedro López presented a petition on August 12, 1553, for the validation (*incorporación*) of his licentiate in medicine, the cloister acceded and set the first Sunday in September "para doctorarse en medicine." (Plaza y Jaén, *Crónica*, I, 46.) Since the index states (*Ibid.*, II, 345) that "Se incorporó de Doctor en Medicina," this, too, in all likelihood, was a case—a very ceremonial case—of validating a European degree. On the other hand, Bachelor Damián de Torres was "given" the licentiate (AGN, Universidad, II, f. 86), after which he was "examined" and "approved" for the degree of doctor of medicine on December 1, 1553 (Plaza y Jaén, *Cronica*, I, 37) and is thereafter listed by Plaza y Jaén as doctor. (For example, see Plaza y Jaén, I, 49.) In any event, the point maketh not the earth to tremble nor the mountains "to skip like young rams."

97 AGI, México, 95, fs. 375v–76. Execución de la sentencia, México, 7 de julio de 1554. See Icaza, *Sucesos reales*, 240–41.

98 AGI, México, 95, f. 376v.

the 1,500 pesos she had spent in his defense[99]—the equivalent of $45,000 in modern terms. The internal evidence is strong that some critical document was missing from the file when the scribe prepared the copy sent to Spain.[100]

99 *Ibid.*, fs. 377–77v., 378v., 379–79v.
100 Though Icaza, *Sucesos reales*, 74–75, and Rodríguez Marín in Menéndez y Pelayo, *Historia de la poesía*, I, 29, n. 1, blandly state that Nava was actually "turned over to ecclesiastical jurisdiction," there is no direct evidence that he actually was or that Viceroy Luis de Velasco or the *oidores* ever commuted the death sentence. Nava's lawyer did tell the royal *audiencia* (AGI, México, 95, f. 376v.) that when Judge Mejía took Nava from the church he promised that he would return "a coat and some breeches of mail," which had not yet been done, and then he adds, rather cryptically, that ". . . by sentence of the vicar-general [*provisor*] of this holy church of Mexico it was commanded that Hernando de Nava be restored to the church with all the rest of the things that were taken from him and the decree [*auto*] was consented [to] and passed as a thing judged. . . ." He did not, however, say whether it was the viceroy and *oidores* who had endorsed this canonical decree, whether it came before or after the amputation of Nava's hand, whether any royal court had granted a commutation of the death sentence, or even whether the body to be "restored" to the church was to be dead or alive—all, perhaps, matters of common knowledge on the streets of Mexico in 1554. He did not even say whether, in fact, the restoration he alluded to had been made. He offered proof—indirect but positive—that in minor matters it had not.

epilogue

D R. PEDRO DE LA TORRE was both a nimble and an instructive fellow. Aside from what they tell of the vicissitudes of a sixteenth-century sinner, the three records of his biography seem just on the verge of pulling back a curtain on the life lived whole by the sons of Conquerors in New Spain. Domestic morality is in a state of suspension as gambling, when the evidence breaks through, becomes the all-but-sole amusement of mature gentlemen who can take marriage or leave it—and often do. The flagrant, show-off heretic gets little more than exile from one town to another. Youths, even when going abroad at night for an ambush, dress like dandies, and when going into society, go accompanied by shield bearers, covered with mail, and armed to the teeth. They quickly and with unremitting and elaborate courtesy make friends with a wandering poet at the inn. Young miscreants address one another decorously as "your worship." A round of baronial dining and ceremonial between families serves to beat off ennui

and to give the feeling of living as hidalgos in the metrop-
olis. In the night, slaves and masters awaken to a cry of
anguish coming from a white man, destined to be a
famous one, and then turn over and go back to sleep because they think they have heard the wails of some "Indians and Negro slaves they were whipping and beating.
. . ." How hard it is to imagine a frontier controlled, as
this one was, by men in velvet and Chinese flowered silk!

In such a society, with nostalgia for the prestige of universities but with little experience of them, the academic
degree all but put a man upon the plane of a Conqueror.
Thus, between the last two episodes in the drama of
Pedro de la Torre, the viceregal authorities had inaugurated a royal and pontifical university in Mexico City that
immediately examined and conferred the degree of doctor of medicine upon the very man who cut off Nava's
hand. With the chance for urbanization and professional
education in a university, all that the men of the new
powerful houses needed to lead a magnificent life was re-
lief from the hovering menace of disease. It took a sweep
of the imagination to bring together the comfort of lux-
ury and the promise of science, but Pedro de la Torre decided to profit by the combination in one bold stroke; he
would confer upon himself the degree of doctor of medicine. Why was such a singular investiture, even when de-
nounced, not fatally dangerous?[1]

Of course, there was a desperate need for doctors, but
concretely, why was De la Torre's claim to be a doctor of
medicine not looked into at Padua? Checking with Euro-

1 The question is critical because modern authorities, in their incidental references to Pedro de la Torre, have naturally taken his personal
investiture as a doctorate from Padua. In such a benign light, unin-
tentional though it may be, the true Pedro de la Torre and his sig-
nificance in American history and medicine cannot be seen properly.

pean universities, especially foreign ones, was so patently difficult and unprecedented in these cases that colonial officials would as likely have thought of checking with heaven. If they had defied heaven, though, they would have found, as I did, that Pedro de la Torre was "non . . . laureato" in the University of Padua.[2] Neither the royal *audiencia* in this case nor the Inquisition in a later arraignment thought of writing to Padua for De la Torre's medical degree. Nor did they venture to ask him when the royal *protomedicato* in Spain examined and licensed him and, with his answer in hand, to write that tribunal to see

2 If the reader will permit me to rise and take the stand in person, I shall humbly confess and duly testify that I have flayed the authorities of Veracruz, the judges of the royal *audiencia* in Mexico, and even the Inquisition, with more feeling than justification, for it was not until I began writing this conclusion that it hit me—almost literally—that after 426 years, I myself should rectify their oversight by appealing to the archivists of Padua. If Pedro de la Torre had no medical degree, I could preen myself upon my acute deductions, or, if he actually was "laureated" with the degree of doctor of medicine, I could dolefully pitch aside my finished manuscript. As I received the answers from Italy, I found myself sinking down onto a bench to recover the strength to read them. Then, after steadying my hand, I opened my eyes to read: Pedro de la Torre was "non . . . laureato" in the University of Padua. From Professor Lucia Rosetti, of the Archivio Antico at the University of Padua, I got this not unexpected, yet reassuring word: "L'Ambasciata d'Italia ci ha trasmesso la sua richiesta . . . riguardante il dottorato in medicina di Pedro de la Torre. Le ricerche condotte nel nostro Archivio hanno dato esito negativo: il de la Torre non risulta laureato presso la nostra Università."

Dr. Elda Martellozzo Forin, of the Instituto di Paleografia e Diplomatico and of the Instituto per la Storia dell' Università di Padova, now working on the "Acta Graduum Academicorum" of the University of Padua, writes me that, "L'Academia Patavina mi ha trasmesso la sua richiesta di notizie sul medico spagnolo Pedro de la Torre e sul suo eventuale dottorato patavino. Ho controllato attentamente l'indice degli *Acta graduum*, ma non appare il nome dello spagnolo. Ho poi chiesto informazioni a una borista del nostro Instituto che sta preparando un ricco articolo sugli scolari spagnoli che frequentarono la nostra Università nella prima metà del secolo XVI: auche la sua risposte è stata negativa. . . ."

if the claim were true. In America, a physician could be as isolated as if, in fact, he were in a new world.[3]

Neither the officials in Mexico nor those in Spain cared enough to act further in this instructive case. The neglect was as good as a pardon for an agile fellow such as De la Torre. Five years after his last "definitive" sentence to exile for using a forged license, he was back in Veracruz, his house his own, his practice flourishing, and his retinue of household slaves and servants as imposing as ever —all without a hint of scandal.

As Pedro de la Torre's career advanced from prosecution in the civil courts for illicit practice of medicine to prosecution in the episcopal Inquisition for a whole battery of offenses, the more passing strange it became. Who would have thought that an adventurer patently guilty of bigamy, blasphemy, and sorcery—not to mention rank theological aberrations—could walk off, all but a free man, from trial by the Holy Inquisition! How incredible, too, that a man claiming the lineage of hidalgo before the Holy Inquisition should not know the name of his own grandfather![4] Equally astonishing is that neither the vicar of Veracruz, where De la Torre had been for nine years, nor Bishop Martín de Hojacastro's *provisor* should have any recollection that, six years before, the defendant had been convicted for presenting a false medical license in that very town. They even expressed puzzlement that a man "with a doctor's degree" should have need to resort

---

3 Apparently only one medical interloper among the untold ones caught up during the colonial period wrote back to Europe, when given a term in which to do so, and substantiated his claims with documents from his university. No man on trial, of course, would himself be so clodpated as to write the university where he never graduated for a certified copy of his diploma.

4 AGN, Inquisición, II, Exp. 13, f. 377. Confesión del Dr. Pedro de la Torre, Ciudad de los Angeles, 5 de noviembre de 1551.

to necromancy to cure the toothache. They ought also to have wondered why De la Torre never once offered to produce documentary proof of his career, especially of his academic degrees. It was just not thinkable that they could produce the record at Padua or perhaps—just perhaps—they felt in their hearts the story of his academic training was false and did not want it to be so.

It is wrong, however, on two scores to say that, as medicine in the sixteenth century was at best still Hippocratic, it made little difference how few licensed doctors there were and how many curers flourished. People then, if anything, had more confidence in physicians than do men today, and second, doctors with their often sound heritage in therapeutics could prevent mistakes in treatment of many diseases that meant the difference between living and dying. Licensed practitioners of all types knew they were in extreme demand. Had it not been so, perhaps Hernán Cortés would not have had to contest a bill presented to him in 1534 by an overly expansive apothecary named Diego Velázquez,[5] enough in itself to draw the hostile attention of the Marquis of the Valley.

Questions introduced into the interrogatory of the Inquisition in 1551 more than intimated that De la Torre's life had been irregular in the extreme. They clearly suggested, for example, that he had entered a religious order. Nothing else, in fact, implied in this interrogation turned out to be false. What was more logical, then, than that he should have studied theology, taken holy orders, or be-

---

5 Leonardo Gutiérrez Colomer, "Del pleito habido entre Hernán Cortés y su farmacéutico (hallazgo de documentos en el Hospital de Jesús, de México)," *Anales de la Real Academia de Farmacia*, XXV (Madrid, 1959), Núm. 1, pp. 41–65. Cortés, not deigning to admit personally that any bill was too high for him, contested the case through his chamberlain.

come a "professed friar"—all of which he was at pains to deny,[6] perhaps to cover his heretical error with the haze of feigned ignorance? More immediate was the need to escape the stigma and risk of becoming a declared renegade. Did he break away? Did the order reject him as unfit? In either case his course was toward adventure and toward America. In answering his questioners, it was natural enough that De la Torre should not allude to Tehuantepec, where he lost his woman in a wager and recovered her with a ransom, or to Coatzacoalcos, where, unless somebody lied under oath, he began to live in carnal knowledge of a minor.

Indeed, if the marital life of Dr. Pedro de la Torre was what it now appears to have been, no wonder that Leonor de Osma was unfaithful! If he had cleaved only unto Luisa, a Spanish poet now famous might have gone on composing his beautiful madrigals for three decades more. Leonor was only twenty-two, "more or less," when her inamorato ambushed Cetina,[7] yet De la Torre, by sworn testimony, had married her in Coatzacoalcos before he came to Veracruz,[8] where he is first found afoul of the law in 1542.[9] At that date she could have been only ten years of age. Even if De la Torre did not marry her before coming to Veracruz in 1541 and if he then swore in 1545, as he did,[10] that he was "a married man, having a wife and an

6 AGN, Inquisición, II, Exp. 13, f. 278. Confesión del Dr. Pedro de la Torre, Ciudad de los Angeles, 5 de noviembre de 1551.
7 AGI, México, 95, fs. 248v.–49. Confesión de Leonor de Osma, Ciudad de los Angeles, 10 de mayo de 1554.
8 AGN, Inquisición, II, Exp. 13, f. 372–72v.
9 De la Torre's statement, after he arrived in Madrid in 1546, that he lived in Veracruz for more than four years and the institution of suit against him there on January 13, 1542, strongly indicate that he was already living in that city in 1541. AGI, Justicia, 199, pp. 2, 5.
10 *Ibid.,* 17.

inhabited house in Veracruz," even then his spouse was not a day over thirteen. Twenty-five years younger than De la Torre and without time or opportunity to form her own character, she gave unto the doctor his own prescription, attaching herself, albeit lightly, first to one and then the other of the proud, idle, and sometimes vicious sons of Cortés' *conquistadores*. The internal evidence suggests that Pedro de la Torre had taken Leonor de Osma and her grandmother Leonor Ramírez into his household when the girl was a mere child—perhaps as an arrangement of convenience for the old woman, adrift in a new and strange land. How long he retained Leonor in the house with his mistress before giving her his exclusive attention, if he ever did, will go down like the lost colony as an historical mystery. On that subject, De la Torre is warily vague.

The crisis brought on by the waylaying of Cetina reveals something subtle and dangerous floating in the air of a colonial city soon after the Conquest. A family, with all its ramifications—by law, by blood, and by friendship —could become a power so great as to foil, and certainly to alarm, the viceregal government itself. Surely it was a special tie that could quickly muster so many men in an intricate and desperate resort to jailbreak the very night after the *alcalde* lodged Nava in jail for a wanton crime. Else, how could a man, living off an *encomienda* and abetted by a dozen prominent citizens, hope to live after he had escaped? How this unembodied force, when joined by the church, might strike the state is shown by the highly apprehensive and extremely quick and determined reaction of the royal *audiencia* back in Mexico City. Bishop Hojacastro could remember the abuses of Nuño de Guzmán, the fight of the Franciscans with the corrupt first *audiencia*—excommunicated by Bishop Zumárraga precisely over the issue of sanctuary—but he could hardly have known, when he dined with Nava in the house of Juan Sarmiento, that his fellow guest would leave the table to commit a stealthy, cowardly, and outrageous crime.

What he did know was that the country had now seen nineteen years of highly competent and conscientious viceregal administration. Yet this very competence, when used to protect Indians or to extend royal authority, could jangle the nerves of the not always solvent Conquerors, their sons, and their neighbors. The new viceroy, Luis de Velasco, though known as "the most prudent," after his arrival in late 1550 did carry out an order of the Council of the Indies that, because their masters did not have adequate titles, freed more than sixty thousand Indian slaves—near a quarter of all those remaining in the Indies.[11] The genius of these first Mexican viceroys was that, though revolt might boil and tremble just beneath the surface, they gave way just enough to avoid catastrophic eruption. When, to reverse the dilemma, giving way invited disaster, they could proceed as in this case with a vigor and speed that electrified everybody around them.

The Cetina case, though illuminating the tug-of-war between spoiled Conqueror and jealous crown, is also plain indication that medical standards, if they had changed at all, had fallen since the Conquest. When summoned, So-and-so Cortés, the man who healed by enchantment,

11 Though the law forbade ordinary Indian slavery, natives captured in armed rebellion were legitimate prizes. A formidable number of such prisoners, for example, became slaves of Viceroy Mendoza's soldiers at the time of the Mixtón War, twelve years before Cetina reached Puebla.

brought an apprentice surgeon—surely less prestigious than he—who did what sewing was done. And so established were conjuring and enchantment (*ensalmo*) as a medical technique, though outlawed since the reign of Ferdinand and Isabella,[12] that Gutierre de Cetina, a Spaniard born, called for "him who heals by enchantment" without a flicker of uncertainty. It is no wonder that of the four legitimate doctors practicing in Mexico City in 1545, half of them at some time or other faced the Mexican Inquisition on charges of witchcraft![13] There was, as yet, no secular agency for all New Spain to regularize the medical professions, despite alternating signs of distress and activity from the municipal council in Mexico City. A conflict did develop in the case, but it was between the church and the civil authorities and not between a nonexistent board of king's physicians and the curers. Thus no one, not even the victim, questioned De la Torre's withdrawal from the Cetina case.

The brilliant literary historian, Francisco A. de Icaza, however, did wonder whether "Dr. de la Torre" knew what he was doing when he refused to treat Cetina, a man wounded in a bloody knifing over the doctor's wife beneath the doctor's window, or whether, in view of the "gravity of the wounds," he simply did not know what to do. Then pensively, but with a tinge of sarcasm, Icaza

12 Miguel Eugenio Muñoz (ed.), *Recopilación de las leyes, pragmáticas reales, decretos, y acuerdos del Real Proto-Medicato* (Valencia: Imprenta de la Viuda de Antonio Bordazar, 1751), Capítulo XIX, párra. único, 355–56.

13 How revealing it is that, when facing the inquisitor on charges of sorcerous enchantment, De la Torre should dismiss them as "neither good nor bad" while Dr. Méndez should make light of them as jokes (*burlas*) and boys' stuff (*niñerías*)—which made their adult victims, as they were the first to see, mere simpletons! AGN, Inquisición, XL, Exp. 3, fs. 11v.–12. Confesión del doctor Cristóbal Méndez, México, 15 de noviembre de 1538.

97

asked: "What was the poor man going to do? He did not know how to kill except with prescriptions: perhaps, perhaps, to leave him to die or to spill blood not with the lance, but with the scalpel and the lancet." There is no indication throughout this whole long file that De la Torre was anything except powerless and ineffectual with Cetina. It does not make much difference whether he wanted the patient to die or not. What Icaza did not know was that De la Torre was no doctor at all and that, intruding into practice, he had elected to become a dignified Latin physician—a man to serve the great houses and not expected to do so menial a chore as sew up a sword cut. Why should he settle for the humble work of a romance surgeon, the only man who ever did anything beyond "enchantment" for Cetina?

How illuminating, though, is this plight! If a young man of thirty-five, singer of madrigals for princesses and the nephew of the *procurador general* for the whole kingdom, resorted to what he blandly—even persistently—called "enchantment" medicine, how hopeless it was for the poor to get doctors trained in the universities, the only ones entitled to practice legally! Moreover, had Cetina been so lucky as to get the services of Dr. de la Torre, he still would have had a fraud for a doctor. The standing of a curer rested more upon common report of his "good hits" than upon a license from any royal *protomedicato*. De la Torre, a peninsular and a white man, vaunting a degree he did not have, was always *"dotor,"* never curer (*curandero*). Any fair man, though, would stipulate, as the lawyers have it, that he could and possibly did know as much medicine as his legally practicing contemporaries, but this tempting whimsy must be kept under control; one illegally practicing empiric in 1541, as Fray Antonio Remesal put it, "could bury more Spaniards in one year than all the wars of New Spain in ten."[14]

Strange commentary it is too that Cetina should fade away, as if by another enchantment, without anybody's knowing when or from what he died. If it is known only that he departed this life sometime between April 19, 1554, and June 5, 1557, he could have died naturally of smallpox, rabies, tuberculosis, or some other disease, dear reader, of thine own choice. If, however, Nava was alive seventeen years after he fell afoul of Cetina,[15] the deduction that, but for his wounds, the poet would also have been alive is logical enough. If, then, Cetina did die of complications of his wound, what precisely did he die of? A crashing cut from the top of the left ear across the cheekbone under the left eye that had the apprentice surgeon picking out pieces—one so big and firmly lodged that he had to leave it—suggests that the blow had broken through the paper-thin bone of the concave orbit and into the brain itself. In such a case, meningitis—inflammation of the meninges enveloping the brain and spinal cord—was bound to follow and, in those days, was bound to be fatal.

There is something in this "metanosis," this reconstruction, however, that does not fit into the history of the patient. Three weeks after the attack, Cetina was so much improved that he gave Bachelor Martínez a spontaneous unfolding of the ambush-attack upon him so simple, so graphic, and so tragic that Aeschylus could not have made

14 *Historia general de las Indias Occidentales, y particular de la gobernación de Chiapa y Guatemala* (2nd edition, 2 vols.; Guatemala, 1932), I, 255, quoted in Joaquín Garcia Icazbalceta, *Obras*, I, 78. See also p. 7, n. 4.

15 Francisco Rodríguez Marín in Menéndez y Pelayo, *Historia de la poesía*, I, 29, n. 1.

it starker. To be sure, this achievement was part genius, but it was part improving health too. De la Torre testified that the wound ran across the face from the top edge of the ear obliquely under the left eye—evidence making it less likely that the crashing stroke had caved in the wall of the socket between the eye and the brain. Yet Dr. Gutiérrez and Diego Cortés, in a medical examination on April 19, the last in this case, reported the superficial head wound as healed and the eye only in a "tolerable state," indicating that the eye socket was still irritated and chronically inflamed. In a day when organic matter—eggs, for example—was pushed into the eye as a cure, such a condition was sure to end not only eventually but soon in the overwhelming appearance of pathogenic bacteria to be carried into the bloodstream by the ample vessels serving the orifice of the eye. Gutierre de Cetina, then, most likely died of septicemia—simple blood poisoning. If he did not die forthwith, he never wrote another verse, at least not one that has come down to posterity. Hernando de Nava, because only those whom the gods love die young, must still have been moving around in 1600, accompanying his outbreaks of temper with a ratchety gesture of his left hand.

As becomes an international confidence man, Dr. Pedro de la Torre, after disappearing from the documents for fourteen years, suddenly loomed up in Mexico City as *protomédico*,[16] that classic medical officer charged with keep-

16 *Actas de cabildo*, VII, 412. Cabildos de 10 y 13 de septiembre de 1568. The minutes of September 10 mention only Dr. de la Torre, but those of September 13 specifically name Dr. Pedro de la Torre. A search of the baptismal records of the Parroquia del Sagrario Metropolitano de Puebla, 1545–91, of other categories of microfilmed documents, and of the onomastic card index of the Instituto de Estudios Históricos (Puebla) turn up nothing on anybody named De la Torre. There is scarcely any possibility that this Dr. Pedro de la Torre was an-

ing watch upon other doctors and with imposing the highest ethical and medical standards upon them.[17] He was sixty-one years old in this year of 1568 when the town council appointed him to take the place of the celebrated Dr. Agustín Farfán who, upon the death of his wife, had become an Augustinian friar.[18] De la Torre, with his honor tarnished in Puebla, had moved on to the capital and was, after his unfailing wont, back again at the crest of his profession.

other physician by the same name. There was, at the time, simply no other Dr. de la Torre moving in the medical circles of the capital or, for that matter, anywhere else in the viceroyalty. (See Appendix V.) The town council of Mexico began the practice of appointing these medical examiners and drug inspectors (*protomédicos*) in 1527.

17 There is no use, alas, to cluck the tongue. None of the thirteen English colonies provided any kind of medical examiners until the French and Indian War was well under way nor any formal medical education until 1765—a century and a half after the beginning of English settlement and only a decade before the outbreak of the Revolution. See Richard H. Shryock, *Medical Licensing in America, 1650–1965* (Baltimore, 1967), 14, 16.

18 Though the minutes of the town council (see n. 16 above) do not tell when Dr. Farfán was appointed, they do say that he was serving with another man, a licentiate of medicine, as *protomédico* in 1568. Farfán was the author of *Tratado breve de medicina* (México, 1579), a work so much in demand that it was republished three times in a generation.

APPENDIX I
confesión del
dr. pedro de la torre, I*

[f. 377] EN LA CIUDAD de los Angeles de la Nueva
España a cinco días del mes de noviembre
del año del señor de mil y quinientos y cincuenta y un
años, el Reverendísimo señor don fray Martín de Hoja
Castro obispo de este dicho obispado de Tlaxcala, por
presencia de mí Blas de Morales notario público apostólico y de la audiencia episcopal del dicho obispado, para
tomar la confesión al dicho doctor Pedro de la Torre,
tomó por acompañados a los muy reverendos padres fray
Juan de Gaona provincial de San Francisco y fray Jordán
de Bustillo prior de Santo Domingo del monasterio de
esta ciudad y al Bachiller don Juan de Velasco maestres-
cuela y provisor del dicho obispado, los cuales y cada uno
de ellos juraron por los Santos Evangelios y sobre ellos y
sobre una señal de la Cruz de guardar secreto y hallarse

* AGN, Inquisición, II, Exp. 13, fs. 377–83. So many scribes with such
diverse and forbidding scripts had a hand in this original inquisitorial process against Pedro de la Torre in 1551–52 that the only sensi-
ble approach is, within limits, to modernize the spelling, accentua-
tion, and punctuation of each one of them.

presentes al tomar de la dicha confesión y hacer lo que
deben y son obligados en semejantes casos y después de
haber jurado, fué llamado el dicho doctor Pedro de la
Torre, del cual fué tomado e recibido juramento en forma
devida de derecho, por Dios y por Santa María y por las
palabras de los Santos Evangelios y sobre una señal de la
Cruz, en que puso su mano derecha corporalmente y después de haber jurado y prometido de decir verdad a la
solución del dicho juramento, dijo: sí juro e amen y por
su señoría reverendísima del dicho señor obispo, ante los
dichos padres provincial y prior y por ante el dicho provisor y por presencia de mí el dicho notario le fueron he-
chas las preguntas que se siguieren.

Fué preguntado como se llama y de donde es natural y
que edad tiene. Dijo que se llama Pedro de la Torre y que
es de edad de cuarenta y cuatro años poco más o menos.

Fué preguntado donde es natural y donde nació. Dijo
que es de Logroño en Castilla y nació en la calle que se
dice la Rorra Vieja.

[f. 377v.] Fué preguntado como se llamaron sus padres
y si son vivos. Dijo que su padre se llamó Lope de Vergara
y su madre María de la Torre y que son fallecidos.

Fué preguntado que diga e declare que parientes tiene y
como se llaman y si son vivos y donde. Dijo que los baro-
nes son sus parientes y no se acuerda bien de ellos, porque
a treinta y cinco años que salió de Logroño y no sabe si
son vivos o muertos.

Fué preguntado si sus padres eran cristianos viejos y
como se llamaron sus abuelos. Dijo que sus padres eran
cristianos viejos y no sabe como se llamaron sus abuelos
y este declarante es cristiano viejo.

Fué preguntado donde ha residido y estado de treinta
años a esta parte. Dijo que [de] edad de siete años salió

de España y fué a Italia y en Roma estudió gramática. Fué preguntado donde estudió la ciencia a que dice que sabe. Dijo que de Roma fué a Bolonia donde estudió Artes cuatro o cinco años y de Bolonia fué a Padua donde estudió medicina seis años.

Fué preguntado si ha estudiado teología y donde la estudió y con quien y que tanto tiempo. Dijo que no ha estudiado teología de propósito, más de que oyó algunas lecciones de Santo Tomás y que la profesión de este declarante era de medicina.

Fué preguntado si ha residido en alguna parte de Alemania o en Basilea y con quien estuvo y a que personas recibió. Dijo que ha estado y residido en la ciudad de Basilea y no se acuerda el tiempo que estuvo en ella y que fué criado de Erasmo Roterodamo y le recibía y recibió de paje y esto fué antes que estudiase artes y medicina, siendo muchacho de pequeña edad.

[f. 378] Fué preguntado que fué la causa que se salió de España y se fué a Italia. Dijo que los padres de este declarante le enviaron a Roma con un tío suyo clérigo que se decía el deán de Villosloda, con el cual fué a Roma.

Fué preguntado si en algún tiempo en Roma o en otra parte recibió y ha recibido orden sacra o si ha sido fraile profeso de alguna orden. Dijo que no es de ninguna orden, ni menos ha sido fraile profeso de ninguna orden, ni por ninguna vía.

Fué preguntado que tantos años a que pasó a esta Nueva España y donde ha residido. Dijo que a diez y seis años poco más o menos que pasó a Santa Marta y a estado en Cartagena y en Santa Marta y en Honduras y que podrá haber ocho o nueve años que pasó en esta Nueva España donde ha estado y residido con su casa y mujer.

Fué preguntado si es verdad que si en la ciudad de la

Veracruz un domingo en la noche que se contaron trece días del mes de septiembre que ahora pasó de este presente año, en presencia de ciertas personas, dijo y sustentó que deus et natura yden [*idem*] sunt. Dijo que es verdad que este declarante en el dicho día que le es preguntado dijo la dicha proposición, diciendo que deus et natura yden sunt, lo cual dijo en presencia de Manuel Griego regidor de la dicha ciudad de la Veracruz y de un Francisco Pérez y de la mujer de Juan López el viejo y de otras personas que estaban presentes, que no se acuerda quien eran. Fué preguntado, diga y aclare sobre que materia dijo la dicha proposición que deus et natura yden sunt. Dijo que entrando este declarante en casa del dicho Francisco Hernández a le visitar este declarante le dijo al dicho Francisco Hernández Dios os de salud, que ahora es tiempo de mostrar vuestro buen ánimo, para lo que Dios ordenare [f. 378v.] y no desconfíes de vuestra salud, porque como quiera que nosotros los médicos no la podemos dar, menos sabemos entender lo que Dios querrá hacer y enfermedades muy más peligrosas que la vuestra, suele Dios maravillosamente obrar, pues en naturaleza conocemos siempre las cosas divinas, así que confiado que Dios que puede, vos dará salud y fué el caso que un médico que dicen llamarse el licenciado Toro, respondió a este declarante, diciéndole señor y a la naturaleza es tan debilitada que no podrá turnar arriba, como del todo dando a entender el dicho Toro que era imposible la salud en el dicho enfermo y este declarante se enojó de oirlo que dicho Toro médico le dijo y a ésto este declarante dijo, de naturaleza propia de Dios es hacer divinas obras y muchas veces las vemos y experimentamos en casos más peligrosos y vemos relucir sus virtudes y deus et natura yden

106

sunt, la cual palabra después que este declarante la dijo, le pareció que causó escándalo en los oyentes y este declarante dice y confiesa que es verdad que la dijo, al mismo sentido católico que en esta confesión dice y dirá. Fué preguntado como y de que manera este declarante entiende la dicha proposición que así dijo, en decir que deus et natura yden sunt, por la afirmó a los circunstantes. Dijo que como este declarante la entendió es que dios y naturaleza divina son una misma cosa, no entendiendo entonces por naturaleza criada, más hablando cuan propio sea de Dios y cuanto de su divina naturaleza hacer [f. 379] cosas excelentes y no pensadas de las criaturas y de esta manera dijo que Dios y naturaleza eran una misma cosa y ahora lo dice así, por que este declarante tiene entendido que Dios y naturaleza divina son una misma cosa y no dos, ni entresi difieren.

Fué preguntado si a la sazón que lo suso dicho se trataba entendía, naturaleza divina, como se atravesó de por medio la flaqueza del enfermo y como cuadraba el argumento que hacía con el dicho médico. Dijo que este declarante no sabe lo que le respondió el dicho médico y que si este declarante habló inconsideradamente no lo entiende, sino como tiene dicho en su confesión.

Fué preguntado que es la causa que después que dijo la dicha proposición y salió de casa del dicho Francisco Hernández, la volvió a reseñar delante de muchas personas, los cuales le pidieron declaración de la dicha proposición y no la dió, antes de nuevo la tornó afirmar y muchas veces diciendo que dicho médico no la entendía, que este declarante la entendía muy bien. Dijo este declarante entendió que Dios y naturaleza divina era una misma cosa y que si este declarante ha dicho que Dios y la naturaleza criada son una misma cosa, lo tiene por herético condenado, lo cual este declarante no ha dicho, ni a este declarante se le pidió declaración de la dicha [f. 379v.] proposición, ni tal cosa se acuerda que se le hubiere pedido por ninguna persona.

Fué preguntado que en que libros de filósofos o gentiles ha leído que deus et natura yden sunt. Dijo que no lo ha leído en ninguna parte, ni tal ha visto.

Fué preguntado que en que parte de Santo Tomás ha leído la dicha proposición. Dijo que no ha leído tal cosa en Santo Tomás, ni de tal sea verdad.

Fué preguntado si lo ha oido predicar en alguna parte, o en algún estudio ha oido decir que deus et natura yden sunt como el lo dijo e afirmó. Dijo que no lo ha oido predicar, ni tal cosa ha oido en estudio, ni en otra parte.

Fué preguntado que cuantos años ha estudiado y estudió de teología y donde. Dijo que dice lo que dicho tiene.

Fué preguntado que es la causa haber dicho y afirmado en la Veracruz, que había estudiado doce años de teología. Dijo que si este declarante dijo tal cosa, que no atentó en ello y que miente y no dijo verdad, porque no estudió de propósito, sino accidentalmente algunas lecciones.

Fué preguntado que pues dice, que no ha leído en Santo Tomás donde diga que deus et natura yden sunt, que como y porque dijo en la ciudad de la Veracruz que lo que decía, en decir que deus et natura yden sunt que Santo Tomás lo decía y que lo sustentaría como lo decía Santo Tomás a todos los que lo quisiesen oir y a todo el mundo. Dijo, que no ha dicho ni dijo tal cosa, ni menos que lo sustentaría por dicho de Santo Tomás.

[f. 380] Fué preguntado si en Santa Marta o en Cartagena o en otra alguna parte ha sido condenado por algún juez eclesiástico, por algunas palabras mal sonantes que ha dicho contra nuestra Santa Fe Católica, o por algunas blasfemias. Dijo que pública y secretamente ha sido castigado por ningún caso, si no ha sido en la ciudad de la Veracruz, que el Vicario Bartolomé Romero le condenó en tres pesos de oro común, porque decían que este declarante había dicho estando jugando en casa de Francisco Hernández con el dicho Francisco Hernández y con Antonio Ruiz, que aunque Dios viniese no le ganaría a la persona con quien este declarante jugaba y por esto le condenó el dicho Vicario como dicho tiene.

Fué preguntado, pues que dice no ha sido condenado por ningún juez, que la causa que a pedimento de Juan de Añasco alcalde mayor que fué de la Ciudad de la Veracruz, se hizo contra este declarante a esta información y se tomó por testigo un padre Dominico que decía que fué el juez que lo sentenció y a un fulano que fué notario de la causa y este declarante supo que se hizo la dicha información contra él. Dijo que la causa por que se hizo o quizo hacer la dicha información, fué porque dicho Juan de Añasco, como enemigo de este declarante, intentó a que se hiciese la dicha información, más que este declarante intentó no sabe si se hizo la dicha información contra él, porque nunca se le demostró tal información, ni supo de ella y este declarante no ha sido castigado, como dicho tiene y esto responde de esta pregunta.

Fué preguntado si sabe y tiene por cierto que la confesión vocal es de jure divino y que él que no se confesare y comulgare en cada un año no cumple con el precepto de la iglesia. Dijo que este declarante tiene por cierto que se han de confesar los cristianos y comulgar en cada [f. 380v.] un año y lo tiene por cosa muy cierta la confesión y comunión, porque él de jure divino y eclesiástico y este declarante lo tiene por obligatorio.

Fué preguntado si la semana Santa de la cuaresma pasada de este año estuvo en el Monasterio de Jalapa, donde esta un monasterio y religiosos o donde la tuvo. Dijo que la Semana Santa estuvo en el camino de México a la Veracruz y llegó al dicho pueblo de Jalapa el segundo día de Pascua de Resurrección o el primero y estuvo en el dicho pueblo de Jalapa dos días de Pascua y de allí salió para la Veracruz. Fué preguntado si tiene por costumbre de fe confesar y comulgar las cuaresmas, como es obligado o si deja pasarlos y se confiesa por premio de la iglesia. Dijo que este declarante ha tenido de costumbre de fe confesar y comulgar por las cuaresmas como es obligado, ecepto una cuaresma que no se confesó hasta el domingo de confirmado y por ello le echaron de pena dos libras de cera blanca.

Fué preguntado si algunas veces ha dicho a su mujer y a la abuela de su mujer y a otras personas queriéndose ir a confesar, que no fuesen, que, que pecados tenían que confesar, esto venídoselo por muchas vías. Dijo que nunca tal ha dicho a ninguna persona.

Fué preguntado si les ha estorbado a los suso dichos, que no fuese a misa. Dijo que nunca tal ha dicho a ninguna persona.

[f. 381] Fué preguntado si los domingos o fiestas de guardar ha dejado de oir misa mayor como es obligado y a los sermones, o si se ha estado jugando a los naipes y ha dejado de ir. Dijo que siempre va a misa mayor y ha ido y a los sermones, si no ha sido por justo impedimento de enfermedad y no de otra manera alguna.

Fué preguntado si ha detenido algunas veces a sus mozos y criados que no vayan a misa o hace confesar. Dijo que nunca tal ha dicho, antes los hace y ha hecho confesar y que vayan a misa.

Fué preguntado si cura con medicinas o con palabras, o

de que manera cura, si tiene algunas ceremonias para curar. Dijo que no ha curado, sino solamente con medicinas y no con otra cosa alguna.

Fué preguntado si teniendo en la mano una espada, hacía poner a algunas personas los dedos sobre las muelas que les dolían y con un alfiler punzaba en la vaina de la tal espada y punzando decía y ha dicho ciertas palabras, diciendo apreta el dedo que no os lo quitare, lo cual ha hecho muchas veces, diga las palabras y ceremonias o superticiones que hacía y ha hecho en lo suso dicho. Dijo que es verdad, que este declarante ha hecho lo contenido en la pregunta cuatro o cinco veces, diciendo perli santima cali y diciendo esto tenía una espada en la mano y en la vaina de ella escribía las dichas palabras y decía al que dolía la muela, que la apretase con el dedo y así hacía lo susodicho.

Fué preguntado que por que usaba las dichas palabras y hacía lo susodicho y si lo tiene por bueno o malo. Dijo que este declarante lo ha usado las dichas veces, más que no sabe si es bueno ni malo y que por lo haber visto a un [f. 381v.] sacristán en la ciudad de Sevilla lo hizo y no por otra cosa, porque este declarante no lo tiene por superticción.

Fué preguntado que diga y declare que eficacia o virtud creía que tenía la espada o vaina de ella, pues que en ella escribía las dichas palabras, que aclaradas tiene. Dijo que este declarante no tomaba la dicha espada porque supiese que en ella había virtud alguna, más de porque se podía escribir en la dicha vaina y por esto escribía en ella las dichas palabras.

Fué preguntado que siendo graduado de doctor en medicina, porque se permitió curar del dolor de las muelas con las palabras y ceremonias susodichas y después curó este declarante con ellas. Dijo que estando este declarante en la dicha ciudad de Sevilla con dolor de muelas, en compañía del dicho sacristán, este declarante se había hecho muchos remedios para el dolor de las muelas y el dicho sacristán le dijo que el se lo quitaría y con una espada diciéndole las dichas palabras le dijo, que apretase el dedo en la muela y lo hizo y a este declarante le pareció que le quitó el dolor de muelas y no le dolió por el presente y otro día de mañana se sacó la muela a hierro y este declarante creyendo que era cosa buena le dejó hacer y así lo ha hecho él algunas veces como dicho tiene y no por otra cosa que mala fuese.

Fué preguntado si estando en la ciudad de la Veracruz en tiempo que Pedro Varela era la vos, este declarante hizo venir [a] una mujer casada a casa del dicho Pedro Varela ciertas noches con arte de nigromancia, la cual estaba con el dicho Pedro Varela y se volvía a casa [f. 382] de su marido, sin que lo sintiese el marido. Dijo que no sabe tal cosa, ni tal ha hecho, ni sabe nigromancia, ni la deprendió, ni la entiende. Fué preguntado que es la causa que se alabó muchas veces de haber el hecho lo contenido en la pregunta. Dijo que nunca de tal cosa este declarante se ha alabado en ningún tiempo.

Fué preguntado si estando jugando a los naipes en casa de Francisco Hernández, vecino de la Veracruz, con un Antonio Ruiz y Pedro Hernández de Burgos y Espinosa y con el dicho Francisco Hernández dijo por una mano que le ganó el dicho Antonio Ruiz, no creo en Dios, si aunque Dios padre baje acá abajo os gane a los naipes. Dijo que no sabe cosa alguna de lo que le es preguntado en esta pregunta y que dice lo que dicho tiene de suso contenido, cerca de esto y que no dijo, ni ha dicho lo contenido en la dicha pregunta, ni la dicha blasfemia y que este declarante hace denuncio ante el dicho vicario de la ciudad de la Veracruz como dicho tiene de lo susodicho, porque le dijeron a este declarante que lo había dicho, más que este declarante como dicho tiene, no ha dicho, ni dijo las dichas blasfemias y este declarante para más satisfacción de la proposición que tiene confesada que deus et natura iden sunt y para conlcuir en ello dice y aclara que si este declarante dijo que deus et natura iden sunt, que le entendió por la naturaleza divina y si de otra manera los circunstantes lo entendieron, pide que sean señalados, porque no es de este declarante decir herejías, pues sus padres eran hidalgos y este declarante lo es y este declarante tiene por diabólica herejía decir que naturaleza criada y Dios sean una misma cosa, pues en infinito digiere, siéndola una miserable infinita posible y Dios poderosísimo infinito im [f. 382v.] posible, empero si menos caute o con el alteración del enojo que este declarante tenía, lo dijo de manera que no lo entendieron los circunstantes, les piden perdón, no porque este declarante los quisiese escandalizar, más del escándalo que ellos tomaron por la falta de las letras que tienen, o por falta de no le entender y resumiéndose de todo lo dicho que este declarante dijo, que de naturaleza de Dios era dar salud al enfermo y Dios y naturaleza era una misma cosa, entendiendo de la naturaleza divina y no por otra cosa, y que este declarante como dicho tiene, tiene por falso y herético, si alguna persona dijere que Dios y naturaleza criada era una misma cosa y que todo lo que dicho tiene es la verdad para el juramento que hecho tiene y en ello se afirma y ratifica y ratificó después de haber sido leído y la firmó de su nombre.

Fué preguntado como se llamaba una india que este declarante tenía en su poder. Dijo que se llamaba Luisa y la conoce.

Fué preguntado que en que parte se casó con la dicha

Luisa, o donde le dió palabra de casamiento. Dijo que no se casó con la susodicha ni se veló con ella.

Fué preguntado si estando en el pueblo de Tehuantepeque este declarante jugó a los naipes a la dicha Luisa, con un fulano Molina y después de haberla jugado, pareció ante Juan de Toledo alcalde mayor del dicho pueblo y le pidió que le mandase volver la dicha india, porque no la había podido jugar, que era su mujer y así lo juró en forma por donde se le mandó volver el dicho alcalde mayor y así lo juró en forma [f. 383] por donde se le mandó volver el dicho alcalde mayor y este declarante la llevó consigo como a su mujer. Dijo que es verdad que este declarante jugó a la dicha Luisa a los naipes con el dicho Molina, el cual se la ganó y después de se la haber ganado este declarante, la tornó a rescatar con ciertas joyas y baratijas y que este declarante no pareció con el dicho alcalde mayor, ni ante otro juez alguno a la pedir, ni menos se casó con la dicha Luisa, ni le dió palabra de casamiento en ningún tiempo y que desde el día que este declarante se desposó con Leonor de Osma, su mujer, tuvo en su poder a la dicha Luisa en compañía de la dicha su mujer hasta que la vendió y que lo que dicho tiene es la verdad y en todo ello se afirmó y ratificó, después de leido y firmólo de su nombre y su señoría reverendísima y los dichos religiosos acompañados y el dicho provisor.

Fray Martín Obispo de Tlaxcala.
Dr. de la Torre. (Rúbrica)
Fray Juan de Gaona. (Rúbrica)
Fray Jordán de Bustillo. (Rúbrica)
El Bachiller Velasco. (Rúbrica)
Pasó ante mí
Blas de Morales. (Rúbrica)
Notario Público Apostólico.

APPENDIX II
el doctor de la torre, su confesión*

[f. 238v.] EDESPUES de lo suso dicho en esta dicha çibdad de los Angeles, jueves diez dias del mes de mayo [f. 239] de mill e quinientos e çinquenta e quatro años el dicho señor doctor Mexia hizo pareçer ante sy al Doctor de la Torre vezino desta çibdad del qual resçibio juramento por Dios e por Santa Maria e por las palabras de los Santos Evangelios e por la señal de la cruz so cargo del qual prometio de dezir verdad e syendo preguntado por el thenor de lo suso dicho. Dixo que lo que sabe es quel domingo de Casymodo en la noche primero dia del mes de abril proximo pasado estando este testigo en su cama y en su casa acostado oyo que llamavan e davan golpes a su puerta e como este testigo desperto e lo oyo se levanto luego e se puso a la ventana a ver quien era e vio que el que llamava hera Francisco de Peralta el qual dixo a este testigo vaya vuestra merçed luego a casa de Andres de Molina que an muerto a Çetina e luego este testigo se

* AGI, México, 95, fs. 238v.–43v.

115

vistio e fue con el dicho Peralta a casa del dicho Andres [f. 239v.] de Molina e hallo quel dicho Gutierre de Çetina tenia una cuchillada muy grande en la cara que le toma desde el canto de la oreja por lo alto della hasta la nariz por debaxo del ojo e ansymismo tenia otra cuchillada en la cabeça de las quales le corria mucha cantidad de Sangre e luego este testigo con Anton Martin çirujano lo curaron e despues de curado pregunto este testigo al dicho Gutierre de Çetina que quien lo avia herido e le rrespondio que no le preguntase cosa ninguna y en esto llego alli Gonçalo Galeote con vn montante en la mano e un capotillo de damasco negro e le pregunto a este testigo que si hera la herida de muerte y este testigo le rrespondio que para que lo queria saber y el dicho Gonçalo Galeote le dixo que por que le ynportava mucho y este testigo le dixo juro a Dios que vos le aveys hecho pues que me preguntays esto e asy se [f. 240] fueron todos aquella noche y este testigo se fue a su casa dexando al dicho Gutierre de Çetina mas por muerto que por bivo por que heran las heridas mortales e otro dia lunes syguiente oyo este testigo dezir publicamente asi a Catalina Velez Rascon madre del dicho Hernando de Nava como a Ana de Nava su hija muger de San Juan de Çuñiga e a Diego de Villanueva e a Hernando de Villanueva e al dicho San Juan de Çuñiga como a otras personas que de sus nonbres al presente no se acuerda que se pusyese rremedio luego que Hernando de Nava en que se pusiese en cobro por quellos tenian por çierto quel dicho Hernando de Nava avia dado las dichas cuchilladas e luego aquel dia Pedro Moreno alcalde prendio al dicho Hernando de Nava e le puso en la carçel publica desta çibdad y aquella noche fue publico e notorio quel dicho [f. 240v.] Hernando de Nava se salio de la carçel e que le ayudaron a salir no sabe este testigo quien ni

que personas le ayudaron ni como se salio e yendo este
testigo otro dia por la mañana despues de herido el dicho
Çetina a visitar a Ysabel Velez su hermana questava en-
ferma le hallo en camisa al dicho Hernando de Nava con
una turca de tafetan morado puesta y este testigo dixo a
la dicha Ysabel Velez no sabeys como se dize por esta çibdad publicamente que vuestro hermano Hernando de
Nava dio la cuchillada a Gutierre de Çetina e que Galeotillo estava con el y el dicho Hernando de Nava dixo a este
testigo luego el que le hirio espantarlo queria por que sy
le quisiera matar bien pudiera y este testigo le dixo bien
creo que deveys de ser vos el que lo hizo pues eso dezis e
no le rrespondio mas y este testigo se salio e no se hablo
mas en ello y despues que vino el dicho señor [f. 241] juez
pesquisidor a esta çibdad el dicho Gonçalo Galeote fue a
casa deste testigo y le dixo señor Doctor por amor de Dios
que sepa sy ay mandamiento contra mi por que yo me
temo que an de prender por que yo fuy el que di la cuchillada en la cabeça al dicho Çetina e tengo su sonbrero
en mi poder e aquel mismo dia que paso esto el dicho señor juez le corrio hasta metello en la yglesia de Santo Domingo y este testigo tiene por çierto que los dichos
Hernando de Nava e Gonçalo Galeote fueron en dar las cuchilladas al dicho Gutierre de Çetina e al dicho Peralta
por quel dicho Galeote se lo dixo a este testigo que le
avian dado siete o ocho heridas al dicho Peralta e que no
sabia como no le avian herido y esto sabe quanto a las
cuchilladas del dicho Çetina y en lo demas dixo que lo que
sabe es que el miercoles proximo pasado bispera de la
Asençion en la noche seria entre la una e las dos oras de
la noche estando este testigo durmiendo en su [f. 241v.]
cama con su muger le vino a dezir Leonor Dosma su muger dando gritos como Hernando de Nava estava alli y

117

que le avia dado una cuchillada en la cara y este testigo
luego se levanto e dio gritos diziendo negros negros y
abrio la puerta de la sala e tomo una lança y al tiempo que
la abrio vio quel dicho Nava se baxava por el escalera
abaxo y este testigo vio que a las bozes que dava salio un
negro suyo que se dize Juan Galan y subio corriendo por
la escalera arriba donde este testigo estava e fue a la cabe-
çera de su cama e tomo una espada deste testigo e se deçendio abaxo y a los gritos queste testigo dava diziendo a
estos traydores el dicho Nava subia por unas paredejas a
las açoteas e vio quel dicho negro Juan Galan le tiro de los
pies e no le dexo subir y luego el dicho Nava se fue para el
dicho negro con la espada en la mano e le tiro muchas cuchilladas y estando en este llego el dicho Gonçalo Galeote
en su favor que estava [f. 242] abajo en el patio e vio este
testigo que dio una cuchillada por detras el dicho Gonçalo
Galeote al dicho Juan Galan negro en el brazo muy grande
de la qual este testigo vio quel dicho negro solto e se le
cayo la espada e se fue luego corriendo a la escalera
donde este testigo estava y en esto salio una negra que se
dize Ceçilia e vio quel dicho Hernando de Nava le dio una
estocada en un muslo e como se vido herida se vino donde
este testigo estava e luego estando de la manera suso dicha vio este testigo que una negra suya que se dize Yseo
deçendio abaxo con las llaves de la puerta la qual sintio
este testigo abrir e começo a dar muy grandes bozes e
gritos en la calle llamando a los vezinos y este testigo vio
que los dichos Hernando de Nava e Gonçalo Galeote como
oyeron abrir la puerta se yvan hazia ella y en esto vio este
testigo que luego entro por la dicha puerta un onbre man-
çebo [f. 242v.] que le pareçio a este testigo que hera Martin de Mafra hermano de Gonçalo Galeote e los llamo a
bozes que se saliesen que la puerta estava abierta e luego

Appendices

los dichos Hernando de Nava e Gonçalo Galeote se salieron fuera a la calle como este testigo los vio fuera baxo
detras dellos e vio que yvan amenazando a este testigo
diziendo todos tres que si salia a la calle que lo avian de
matar y otras amenazas e palabras feas e vio que se
yvan hazia el monesterio de Santo Domingo e oyo luego
llamar muy apriesa a la canpanilla de la porteria e como
este testigo vio que ya se avian ydo se fue a casa del señor
juez pesquisidor e lo llamo e vinieron el y su escriuano e
alguazil e hallaron al dicho negro e negra e a su muger
Leonor Dosma con sendas cuchilladas en las partes e
lugares que dicho tiene y despues de [f. 243] aver hecho
ynformaçion se fue a Santo Domingo y despues de la aver
visto los frayles abrieron las puertas y entro el dicho señor juez e mucha gente e se fue a la torre donde hallo
fortaleçidos a los dichos Hernando de Nava e Gonçalo
Galeote y a este testigo le paresçe quel dicho Mafra estava
con ellos y no sabe este testigo que otras personas estuvie-
sen en la dicha Torre ni que oviesen ydo a casa deste testigo con los dichos Hernando de Nava e Gonçalo Galeote
e Martin de Mafra a cometer los dichos delitos y este testigo sabe e vio quel dicho dia miercoles en la tarde bispera de la Asençion a boca de noche e muy tarde los
dichos Hernando de Nava e Gonçalo Galeote estavan en el
monesterio de Santo Domingo retraydos por queste testigo los vio e sabe que avian estado alli çiertos dias avia
retraydos por las cuchilladas del dicho Çetina y esto es lo
que [f. 243v.] sabe deste caso y es la verdad para el juramento que hizo e fuele leydo e retificose en el e firmolo de
su nonbre e que este testigo es de hedad de mas de qua-
renta años e que avnque a este testigo le toca por eso no
a dexado de dezir verdad a la qual ayude Dios e al que
tuviere justiçia testigos que fueron presentes al jura-

119

mento suso dicho Diego de Hojeda e Juan Mendez de Rosas e Alonso de Tarifa estantes en esta çibdad de los
Angeles el Doctor de la Torre anti mi: Juan de Guevara escriuano.

APPENDIX III
confesión de francisco, negro esclavo*

[f. 284]   E DESPUES de lo suso dicho en esta dicha çibdad de los Angelez onze [f. 284v.] dias del mes de mayo e del dicho año de mill e quinientos e çinquenta e quatro años el dicho señor oydor hizo pareçer ante si a Francisco negro esclavo que dixo ser del dicho Hernando de Nava del qual fue recibido juramento por Dios e por Santa Maria e por las palabras de los Santos Evangelios e por la señal de la cruz so cargo del qual prometio de dezir verdad testigos Juan Mendez de Rosas e Rodrigo del Rio e Luys de la Loa estantes en esta çibdad e syendo preguntado por lo contenido en este proçeso dixo que sobre lo que les preguntado este testigo tiene dicho su dicho antel juez pesquisidor e ante mi el dicho escriuano el qual tiene dicho e declarado la verdad e pidio le fuese leydo e yo el dicho escriuano se lo ley de berbo ad verbum como en el se contiene que le fue tomado en vey-

* AGI, México, 95, fs. 284-92v.

121

nte e vn dias del mes de abril e dixo que en el se rretificava e retifico e afirmava e afirmo e si hera neçesario lo tornava e torno [f. 285] a dezir agora de nuevo en esta cabsa e no tiene mas que dezir e que esta es la verdad e lo que sabe deste caso para el juramento que hizo e fuele leydo e rretificose en el e no firmo por que dixo que no sabia escrevir e lo firmo el dicho señor oydor e queste testigo es de hedad de doze años poco mas o menos e que no le enpeçen las generales e que Dios ayude a la verdad paso ante mi: Juan de Guevara escriuano. E luego yncontinente el dicho señor oydor dixo que atento la calidad del caso e queste es esclavo y domestico del dicho Hernando de Nava que para mejor saber la verdad le mandava poner a question de tormento e luego fue puesto en el burro el dicho Francisco e atadas las manos e puestos çiertos cordeles a los pies e braços e puestos garrotes en los cordeles para dar buelta e le fue encargado que diga la verdad dixo que lo quite de alli quel dira la verdad de lo que pasa e luego el dicho señor oydor torno [f. 285v.] a dezir al dicho Francisco que en el dicho burro diga la verdad de lo que sabe e syno que alli a de estar e le fueron dadas dos bueltas a los garrotes e apretar los braços y el dicho Francisco dixo que so cargo del juramento que tiene hecho el dira la verdad de todo lo que en el caso pasa y estando en el burro de la manera suso dicha dixo que so cargo del dicho juramento que lo que pasa e sabe destos casos es quel Domingo en la noche quando hirieron al dicho Çetina que avia casy mes e medio el dicho Hernando de Nava e Gonçalo Galeote e Pedro Paez juntaron en la calle y estuvieron hablando para que fuesen a matar al dicho Gutierre de Çetina e Francisco de Peralta porque pasavan por la calle del doctor de la Torre y señaladamente el dicho Martin de Mafra que tanbien se avia juntado e tratado esto

con ellos dixo juro a Dios que los tengo de matar pues que
me an corrido tres o quatro noches y esto este testigo lo
sabe [f. 286] e vio porque se hallo presente por quel dicho
Hernando de Nava le llevava consigo para que mirase la
gente e fuese espia y este testigo llevava vna rodela y vn
caxco la rrodela para el dicho Pedro Paez y el caxco para
Hernando de Nava y el dicho Hernando de Nava yva ar-
mado con una cota e vnos çaraguelles e vn montante e
caxco que despues le tomo a este testigo y llevava vnas
calças blancas y vn jubon blanco y al capote deste testigo
e despues de lo aver todos ellos conçertado buen rato
junto al corral de Hernando de Villanueva ques çerca de
la casa del doctor de la Torre el dicho Pedro Paez tomo
la rrodela a este testigo y el dicho Nava el caxco y este testigo yva junto con ellos e le dixeron que mirase sy venia
alguien e se adelanto este testigo e vio venir al dicho Çetina e Peralta e les conoçio que venian tañendo e dio aviso
a los dichos Nava e sus conpañeros los quales se pusyeron
alli a la [f. 286v.] esquina del dicho corral ques casy fron-
tero de la casa del dicho doctor de la Torre a aguardarlos
e como llegaron el dicho Çetina e Peralta el dicho Nava
dixo no venga vuestra merçed essotilo que yo me quiero
adelantar e dalles e asy se adelanto e dio el dicho Nava al
dicho Çetina vna cuchillada por la cara que le derribo en
el suelo con el dicho montante e despues de caydo el
dicho Galeote con el montante dio al dicho Çetina vna
cuchillada en la cabeça y este testigo lo vio e se hallo presente e despues desto dexaron al dicho Çetina caydo e se
fueron tras del dicho Peralta el qual yva huyendo e le
alcançaron e le dieron muchos golpes en el suelo porque
avia caydo e ponia la espada delante y davan en ella y
entonçes dixo el dicho Hernando de Nava sy yo quisiese
matar vos bien podria e despues desto se fueron hazia

123

Santo Domingo e bolvieron a casa de Juan Sarmiento todos y esto paso despues de aver çenado el obispo con el qual avia çenado el dicho Nava en casa de Juan Sarmiento [f. 287] e antes de çenar avia salido otra vez de casa el dicho Nava e avia buelto y despues de aver dado las dichas cuchilladas mandaron a este testigo que se adelantase e que mirase no pareçiese alguien e venian hablando cosas que este testigo no entendio e al tiempo de las cuchilladas de Peralta el dicho Martin de Mafra y el dicho Galeote juntamente con el dicho Nava todos davan en el dicho Peralta de cuchilladas y despues que llegaron a casa del dicho Juan Sarmiento se fueron el dicho Pedro Paez y el dicho Martin de Mafra e se quedo con el dicho Nava el dicho Gonçalo Galeote e Martin de Soseguera que no avia salido de casa y mando el dicho Nava a este testigo que le hiziese la cama y el dicho Nava delante deste testigo dixo al dicho Gonçalo Galeote vaya vuestra merçed e mire como esta Çetina e asi el dicho Galeote fue e bolvio diziendo que ya avian ydo a llamar quien le curase.

Fue preguntado como tiene dicho en el dicho su dicho antes deste que no salio de [f. 287v.] casa por quel dicho Nava se lo avia mandado y le avia aguardado hasta que bolviese dixo que la verdad es lo que agora tiene dicho e dize e la cavsa por que entonçes dixo no aver salido de casa fue por que Juan Sarmiento e San Juan de Çuñiga le dixeron a este testigo que no lo dixese e para ello les hizieron muchas amenazas diziendo que lo avian de pringar e matar y ansimismo el dicho Hernando de Nava amenazo a este testigo asimismo sobre ello e le dio muchos moxicones e golpes y le pringo e quemo todo el cuerpo espeçialmente las nalgas que tiene muy quemadas e que por miedo que de los suso dichos tenia no oso dezir entonçes todo lo que sabia e que agora a dicho e dize e

dira la verdad de todo e que quando los dichos Hernando
de Nava e Gonzalo Galeote e los demas venian la dicha
noche a dar las cuchilladas a Gutierre de Çetina e Peralta
que venia este testigo con ellos como dicho tiene el dicho
negro Anton [f. 288] esclavo de Juan Sarmiento les abrio
la puerta y entonçes subieron los que dicho tiene y despues desto estando el dicho Hernando de Nava en la carçel preso sobre las dichas cuchilladas el segundo dia que
entro en la carçel por la noche se salio de la carçel e la
manera que tuvieron para ello fue esta que Hernando de
Villanueva yva y venia en casa de Juan Sarmiento y alli
hablavan el y el dicho Juan Sarmiento e San Juan de Çuñiga e Martin de Oseguera sobre el sacar de la carçel al
dicho Hernando de Nava e tanbien yvan alla sobre esto
Diego de Hojeda e Francisco de Reynoso e Diego de Villanueva e Juan de Cisneros mestizo e que conçertaron en
diversas vezes de le sacarse la carçel al dicho Nava e ansimismo fue en ello Carvallar que por otro nonbre se
llama Mansilla e conçertose tambien quel Martin de Oçeguera traxese los mecates y hecho este [f. 288v.] conçierto
aquella noche vino Hernando de Villanueva a la carçel e
dixo al dicho Nava mira no nos angañeys que esta noche
os hemos de sacar a lo qual todo que dicho es este testigo
se hallo presente e antes desto el San Juan de Çuñiga avia
dicho hartos somos para sacarlo de la carçel e poco antes
que lo sacase por la callejuela por detras de la carçel subieron por las açoteas della en lo alto Caravallar Mançanilla e Juan de Çisneros mestizo e Gonçalo Galeote e
quedaron abaxo aguardando Martin de Mafra e Francisco
de Reynoso e Diego de Hojeda e San Juan de Çuñiga e
Juan Sarmiento se quedo en casa y en esto entraron en la
carçel Hernando de Villanueva primero y despues Martin
de Oçeguera a çenar con el dicho Hernando de Nava y el

dicho Oçeguera çeno con el y el Hernando de Villanueva
no comio mas de un bocado [f. 289] y el dicho Villanueva
y el dicho Oçeguera hablavan con el Nava conçertando de
sacallo de la carçel y en esto entro Flores alguazil e ally
desde la dicha carçel con el qual hablo el dicho Nava
aparte e no sabe este testigo lo que hablaron porque no lo
entendio e luego se salio el dicho Oçeguera de la carçel e
se fue a juntar con los otros que dicho tiene questavan
aguardando a la callejuela detras de la carçel e desde a vn
poco salio Hernando de Villanueva hablando con el dicho
Flores hazia la puerta de la dicha carçel e dexo las puertas
donde el dicho Nava estava abiertas y en esto el dicho
Nava se quito los grillos e tomo el hierro grande en la
mano de los dichos grillos e dixo que sy alguien venia
para el que le avia de dar con el e quitoseles facilmente
por que la primera noche que estuvo en la carçel se quito
la chaveta de hierro e se puso vna de çera delante deste
testigo y [f. 289v.] hecho esto mientras el dicho Flores
alcayde abria la puerta de la calle al dicho Hernando de
Villanueva el dicho Nava se salio al patio de la carçel
donde los que dicho tiene questavan en la açotea le acha-
ron vna soga e le subieron a lo alto y este testigo lo vio e
se hallo presente a todo ello y en esto los yndios questavan en el patio dieron bozes al alcayde que se yva Nava e
luego, a las dichas bozes salio este testigo a la calle por
que la puerta della estava abierta como el dicho Flores
dava bozes e se fue derecho a la calligeta donde sabran
questavan aguardando y este testigo vio como el dicho
Nava e los demas que estavan en lo alto baxaron de priesa
por el mecate e los que dicho tiene les recogeron e se fueron huyendo a su gusto domingo e que la otra vez que
dixo su dicho no oso dezir quien heran los suso dichos ni
lo que aqui a dicho por los golpes que le avian dado e

miedo que tenia como dicho tiene e despues desto estando
[f. 290] el dicho Nava e Galeote e Mafra retraydos en
Santo Domingo el miercoles bispera de la Asençion como
este testigo yva y venia a Santo Domingo y llevava de
comer al dicho Nava este testigo vio que los dichos Hernando de Nava e Gonçalo Galeote e Mafra conçertaron de
salir aquella noche e a cuchillar a la muger del doctor de
la Torre y este testigo lo via y entendia y le mandaron que
saliese con ellos por espia para la gente que pasase e vio
como salieron por una pared del corral del dicho monesterio y este testigo con ellos e fueron hazia casa del doctor de la Torre e un onbre venia por la calle y el dicho
Nava se abaxo para que no lo conoçiese e asy paso el dicho onbre e desde alli se fueron a casa del dicho doctor e
subieron por detras por junto dondesta vna ventana [f.
290v.] de vna rexa y el dicho Mafra se quedo aguardando
a la esquina y el dicho Hernando de Nava subio primero
e luego Galeote e luego subieron ellos dos a este testigo y
le mandaron que entrase dentro con ellos para que mirase
no anduviesen por alli algunos negros y esto seria a la
media la noche poco mas o menos e metieron a este testigo delante y luego entraron ellos y el dicho Nava subio
arriba por la escalera a vna ventana que tiene vna rexa
baxa y este testigo subio delante para ver si estava el doctor o alguien e como no vio a ninguna persona dixo a su
amo que subiese e luego subio el dicho Nava e hallo la
ventana çerrada y el dicho Nava llamo con la mano e
luego salio la muger del dicho dotor e abrio media ventana e dixo quien esta ay negro y el dicho Nava luego le
dio una cuchillada por la cara con una daga que llevava
[f. 291] en la mano por entre la dicha rrexa e luego la dicha Leonor Dosma dio bozes e salio el dicho doctor de la
Torre e un negro el doctor con una lança en la mano y el

127

negro con vna espada y el dicho Galeote estava abaxo que
se avia quedado abaxo mientras el dicho Nava avia subido
y el dicho negro tiro çiertos golpes con la espada hazia
donde estava el dicho Nava el qual con un montante dio
al dicho negro que se llama Juan Galan vna gran cuchillada en el braço derecho e a vna negra que se llama Ceçilia dio vna estocada por el muslo e luego una negra que
se llama Yseo abrio la puerta de la calle y salieron el dicho Nava y el dicho Galeote y este testigo a la calle e se
fueron e se anduvieron paseando vn rrato e tornaron a
bolver por alli e luego se fueron a la porteria de Santo
Domingo y llamaron e les abrio vn frayle y entraron dentro e se acostaron y este testigo con ellos e demas desto
este testigo sabe que a muchos dias [f. 291v.] que Yseo
negra esclava de la dicha Leonor Dosma yva e venia con
cartas al dicho Nava y cree este testigo que lo que a hecho
el dicho Nava a sido de çelos y estando retraydo el dicho
Nava en Santo Domingo la dicha Yseo negra yva e venia a
le hablar al dicho Nava por la puerta de la carreteria questa detras del monesterio e que aquella noche que conçertaron e salieron del monesterio a dar la cuchillada a la
dicha Leonor Dosma el dicho Nava dezia asiendose de las
barbas aquella puta que no a de aprovechar nada con ella
que se a de echar con todos ella me lo pagara dexame y
esto dezia delante del dicho Gonçalo Galeote e luego salieron a dar las dichas cuchilladas como dicho tiene e questa
es la verdad so cargo de juramento que tiene fecjo e no
firmo por que dixo que no sabia escrevir e lo firmo el dicho señor oydor e queste testigo es de hedad de doze años
poco mas o menos y luego [f. 292] por el dicho señor oydor fue mandado quitar del burro y desatar los pies y
manos y el dicho Francisco negro torno a dezir questo
que aqui tiene dicho es la verdad e ansimismo todo lo que

Appendices

antes de agora tiene declarado es la verdad e lo que pasa
en quanto lo que no es en contrario desto e fuele tornado
a leer e declarar todo lo suso dicho y el dicho dicho e dixo
que aquello es la verdad para el juramento que lo tiene
hecho e para que conste como fue açetado e pringado por
lo que dicho tiene mostre el cuerpo e nalgas e pareçieron
en el muchas llagas señales e azotes e quemaduras e otros
muchos labores testigos que fueron presentes a lo que
dicho es Luys de la Lea e Rodrigo del Rio estantes en esta
dicha çibdad a los quales les fue tomado juramento en
forma e so cargo del les fue encargado el secreto dixeron
que ansi lo haran y el dicho señor e por si [f. 292v.] lo se-
ñalo paso ante mi Juan de Guevara escriuano.

129

APPENDIX IV
confesión de yseo, negra*

[f. 293v.] **E**LUEGO yncontinente [en esta dicha çibdad de los Angeles onze dias del mes de mayo de mill e quinientos e çinquenta e quatro años] fue trayda la dicha Yseo negra e conforme al dicho auto estando en la dicha carçel fue [f. 294] atada con cordeles los brazos e pies e puesta en el burro y estando de la manera suso dicha le fue tomado juramento en forma por Dios e por Santa Maria e por las palabras de los Santos Evangelios e por la señal de la cruz so cargo del qual le fue encargado que dixese la verdad de lo que sabe de lo suso dicho dixo que para el juramento que hecho tiene lo que tiene dicho en el dicho su dicho es la verdad e lo fue mandado apretar los cordeles e se dieron çiertas bueltas e dadas la dicha Yseo dixo quella dira verdad e syendole preguntado dixo que todo lo que dicho tiene es verdad e que demas desto este testigo sabe e a visto quel dicho Hernando de Nava a ydo muchas vezes de dia e de noche a su casa de su ama desta declarante e a hablado con ella y entre otras cosas

* AGI, México, 95, fs. 293v.–95.

130

le a rreñido muchas vezes por que a ydo e va en casa de
Lazaro de la Roca ques [f. 294v.] junto a vna casa adonde
bivia vn Peralta teniendo çelos del dicho Peralta e aliende
desto la mandava que no saliese de su casa ni fuese a ningun cabo sin liçençia del e que esta testigo via que aunque
el dicho doctor mandava a la dicha su muger que se fuese
a holgar a alguna parte ella no osava por temor que tenia
del dicho Hernando de Nava e que esta testigo nunca
llevo cartas al dicho Hernando de Nava de su ama ni del
para ella avnque por mandado de la dicha su ama le fue a
visitar algunas vezes a Santo Domingo por una puerta
trasera e que demas desto sabe questando retraydo el
dicho Nava en Santo Domingo por las cuchilladas de Çetina la dicha su ama y el se hazian señas ella desde su ventana y el desde la torre e no sabe lo que se dezian e que la
cavsa porquel dicho Nava hirio a la dicha su ama [f. 295]
este testigo no lo sabe mas de que despues de herida la dicha Leonor Dosma dixo a este testigo como el dicho Nava
avia venido a hablar con ella el miercoles en la noche
bispera de la Açension e que despues de aver hablado un
rrato por la ventana de la rrexa ella estava algo apartada
por de dentro y el la tenia por las manos por de fuera e
quella le contava como su marido reñia con ella y el le
rrogava que se llegase mas a la rreja e se quito el dicho
Nava las armas que llevava e casco e guantes e lo puso
ençima de un poyo e aparador e como ella se llegase luego
a lar rreja el dicho Nava le avia dado luego la dicha cuchillada e que se la dio segun dicho tiene e que esta es la
verdad para el juramento que hizo e fuele leydo e rretificose en el e no firmo porque dixo que no sabia escrevir y
el dicho señor oydor la mando des [f. 295v.] ligar e que se
fuese en casa de su amo e lo firmo de su nonbre el dicho
señor oydor testigos Rodrigo del Rio e Luys del Alba ante
mi: Juan de Guevara escriuano.

131

APPENDIX V
pedro de la torre: protomédico*

CABILDO de viernes a diez de setiembre de 1568 años

En este dicho dia mes e año los dichos señores mexico dixeron que por quanto por esta dicha ciudad estaba señalado y nonbrado juntamente con el dotor toro el dotor farfan para que tubiesen quenta con los demas medicos e cirujanos e otras personas que entienden en curar de las enfermedades desta dicha ciudad y en otras cosas como se contiene en el nonbramiento que sobre ello se yzo e por el dicho doctor farfan se ha metido frayle en el monasterio y horden de señor san agustin desta dicha ciudad de mexico de cuya cabsa los dichos señores mexico dixeron que nonbraban y nonbraron al dotor de la torre juntamente con el dicho doctor toro y por el tienpo questa por correr del tienpo para que fue nonbrado el dicho doctor farfan el qual parecia a la acetar a azer sobrello el juramento e solenidad que de derecho es obligado. . . .

* *Actas de cabildo*, VII, 413.

Cabildo de lunes a trece de setiembre de 1568 años

Este dia parecio el dicho doctor pedro de la torre e aceto el dicho nonbramiento y juro a Dios Nuestro Señor de husar bien e fiel y diligentemente dello.

APPENDIX VI
bishop hojacastro
commutes a sentence

1 The said lord bishop, having seen all the abovesaid, said
2 that in the form of petition or as the principal judge in the
3 cause, or as best conforms to law, said that he was commuting
4 and thereby did commute the place where it is ordered by the said
sentence
5 that the said doctor Pedro de la Torre do and say
6 the words touching the said proposition and where it says in the
7 church it should be in the public plaza in this said city in
8 the presence of the royal governor and alcaldes in ordinary and
aldermen
9 and of the persons before whom he spoke the said words
10 of proposition in the manner and as is contained in the sentence
11 and thus also respecting the exile, that he was giving and thereby
did give him license
12 that he might go to the city of Veracruz
13 and be in it and arrange whatever is convenient for him for the time
14 and space of thirty days and no more and in all the
15 rest he was confirming and did thereby confirm the said sentence
16 and ordered that it be kept and obeyed as therein stated.
17 Witnesses: Juan Sarmyento
18   Johan Ruis
19   notario [rúbrica]
20 On Saturday, tertia [at three], the twenty-third of January of fifteen and
21 fifty-two years, being in the jail of his most reverend lordship,
22 I did read and make known the said command of his most reverend
23 lordship to Pedro de la Torre
24 in person, who said that he was consenting and thereby did consent
to
25 all and to the said sentence and will obey all as
26 his lordship commands and the said sentence contains: Witnesses:
Juan
27 Garçia Sorrito and Miguel Blanco
28   Johan Ruis
29   notario [rúbrica]

134

1 El dicho señor obispo, aviendo visto todo lo suso dicho, dixo
2 que en grado de supliçacion o como jues prinçipal en la
3 cabsa o como mejor a lugar de derecho, dixo que comutava
4 e comuto el lugar a donde por la dicha sentençia se manda

5 que el dicho dotor Pedro de la Torre haga e diga las
6 palabras cabe de la dicha propusysion, que como dize en la
7 yglesia sea en la plaça publica de la dicha çibdad en
8 presençia del alcalde mayor e alcaldes hordinarios e regidores

9 e de las personas ante quien dixo las dichas palabras
10 de propusysion en la manera e como en la sentençia se contiene;
11 e asy mismo en quanto al destierro que le dava e dio lizençia

12 que pueda yr a la dicha çibdad de la Veracruzt
13 y estar e negoçiar en ella lo que convenga por tienpo
14 e espaçio de treynta dias e no mas; e en todo lo
15 demas confirmava e confirmo la dicha sentençia
16 e mando que se guarde e cunpla como en ella se contiene.
17 Testigos: Juan Sarmyento
18   Johan Ruis,
19   notario [rúbrica]
20 En sabado, terçia, veynte e tres de henero de quinientos e

21 cinquenta e dos años, estando en la carçel de su señoria reverendi-
                                                              sima,
22 ley e notifique el dicho mandado de su señoria
23 reverendisima de suso al dicho dotor Pedro de la Torre
24 en persona, el qual dixo fue le consentya e consyntio

25 todo e la dicha sentençia e lo conplira todo como su
26 señoria manda e la dicha sentençia contiene. Testigos: Juan

27 Garçia Sorrito e Miguel Blanco
28   Johan Ruis,
29   notario [rúbrica]

135

APPENDIX VII
"they have killed cetina"

1   of one thousand five hundred and fifty and
2   four years the said lord doctor Me-
3   xia had appear before him Doctor
4   de la Torre freeman of this city to
5   whom he administered the oath by God and by
6   Holy Mary and by the words
7   of the Holy Gospels and
8   by the sign of the cross in fear
9   of which he promised to tell the truth
10   and being asked about the
11   tenor of the abovesaid, he said that
12   what he knows is that on the First Sunday
13   after Easter on the night of the first
14   day of the month of April last past
15   this witness being in bed and in
16   his house asleep he heard that they were call-
17   ing and rapping at his door
18   and as this witness awakened and
19   heard it he got right up and went
20   to the window to see who it was and saw
21   that he who was calling was Francisco de
22   Peralta who said to this witness
23   go your worship right away to the house of Andres
24   de Molina that they have killed Cetina and
25   presently this witness dressed and went with the
26   said Peralta to the house of the said Andres

1 de mill e quinientos e çinquenta e
2 quarto años el dicho señor doctor Me
3 xia hizo pareçer ante sy al doctor
4 de la Torre vezino desta çibdad del
5 qual resçibio juramento por Dios e por
6 Santa Maria y por las pala
7 bras de los Santos Evangelios e
8 por la señal de la cruz so cargo
9 del qual prometio de dezir verdad
10 e syendo preguntado por el
11 thenor de lo suso dicho. Dixo que
12 lo que sabe es quel domingo
13 de Casymodo en la noche primero
14 dia del mes de abril proximo pa
15 sado estando este testigo en su cama y en
16 su casa acostado oyo que lla
17 mavan e davan golpes a su puer
18 ta e como este testigo desperto e lo
19 oyo se levanto luego e se puso
20 a la ventana a ver quien era e vio
21 que el que llamava hera Francisco de
22 Peralta el qual dixo a este testigo
23 vaya vuestra merçed luego a casa de Andres
24 de Molina que an muerto a Çetina e
25 luego este testigo se vistio e fue con el
26 dicho Peralta a casa del dicho Andres

137

bibliography

Archival Sources

ARCHIVO GENERAL DE INDIAS

Justicia, Legajo 199.
El Dr. Pedro de la Torre, médico y vecino de México, con el fiscal de S. M. sobre denunciación de su oficio por no tener el título correspondiente. México. Año de 1545.

Audiencia de México, Legajo 95.
Proceso hecho de oficio contra Hernando de Nava, vecino de la Ciudad de los Angeles sobre pendencia en que hizo efusión de sangre. Año de 1554.

ARCHIVO GENERAL DE LA NACIÓN (MÉXICO)

Inquisición, Vol. II, Expediente 13
Proceso formado en la Veracruz en tiempo del Ilmo. Sr. Dn. Fr. Martín Hojacastro, obispo de Tlascala, contra el Doctor Pedro de la Torre sobre las palabras de blasfemia que dijo, y haber dicho que Dios y naturaleza son una misma cosa. Año de 1551.

Inquisición, Vol. XL, Expediente 3
Proceso del Santo Oficio [del señor Arzobispo de México el

138

Bibliography

señor Zumárraga] contra el doctor Méndez, supersticioso. Año de 1538.

Universidad, Vol. II
Cátedras y claustros, 1553–61.

Printed Sources

Actas de cabildo del ayuntamiento de México. 54 vols. México, 1889–1916.

Hazañas y la Rua, Joaquín, ed. *Obras de Gutierre de Cetina.* 2 vols. Sevilla: Imprenta de Francisco P. Díaz, 1895.

Icaza, Francisco A. de, ed. *Conquistadores y pobladores de Nueva España: Diccionario autobiográfico sacado de los textos originales.* 2 vols. Madrid: Imprenta de "El Adelantado de Segovia," 1923.

Nueva Recopilación (Recopilación de las leyes destos reynos. . . .). 3 vols. Madrid: Por Catalina de Barrio y Angulo, 1640.

Plaza y Jaén, Cristóbal Bernardo de la. *Crónica de la Real y Pontificia Universidad de México.* Versión paleográfica, proemio, notas y apéndice de Nicolás Rangel. 2 vols. México: Universidad Nacional de México Autónoma, 1931.

Recopilación de leyes de los reynos de las Indias. 4 vols. Madrid: Por Antonio de Balbas, 1756.

Authorities

Borah, Woodrow, and Sherburne F. Cook. *The Aboriginal Population of Central Mexico on the Eve of the Spanish Conquest [Ibero-Americana, No. 45].* Berkeley: University of California Press, 1963.

Bravo Ugarte, José. *Diócesis y obispos de la iglesia mexicana (1519–1965), con un apéndice de los representantes de la S. Sede en México y viceversa.* México: Editorial Jus, 1965.

Fernández del Castillo, Francisco. "El poeta Gutierre de Ce-

Bibliography

tina y los médicos." I [Notas para la historia de la medicina en México durante el siglo XVI]. *El médico*, Año 11, No. 3 (junio de 1961), 46–50, No. 4 (julio de 1961), 59–64.

García Icazbalceta, Joaquín. *Obras.* I. México: Victoriano Agüeros, Editor, 1905.

Gibson, Charles. *Tlaxcala in the Sixteenth Century.* New Haven: Yale University Press, 1952.

Greenleaf, Richard E. *The Mexican Inquisition in the Sixteenth Century.* Albuquerque: University of New Mexico Press, 1969.

Gutiérrez Colomer, Leonardo. "Del pleito habido entre Hernán Cortés y su farmacéutico (hallazgo de documentos en el Hospital de Jesús, de México)." *Anales de la Real Academia de Farmacia*, XXV, Madrid, 1959, Núm. 1, pp. 41–65.

Icaza, Francisco A. de. *Sucesos reales que parecen imaginados de Gutierre de Cetina, Juan de la Cueva, y Mateo Alemán.* Madrid: Imprenta Fortanet, 1919.

Lanning, John Tate. "The Illicit Practice of Medicine in the Spanish Empire in America." *Homenaje a don José María de la Peña y Cámara (Colección Chimalistac de Libros y Documentos acerca de la Nueva España*, Serie José Porrúa Turanzas, 3). Madrid, 1969, pp. 144–59.

Menéndez y Pelayo, Marcelino. *Historia de la poesía hispanoamericana [Obras completas del Excmo. Señor Don Marcelino Menéndez y Pelayo].* 2 vols. Madrid: Librería General de Victoriano Suárez, 1911–13.

Muñoz, Miguel Eugenio, ed. *Recopilación de las leyes, pragmáticas reales, decretos, y acuerdos del Real Proto-Medicato.* Valencia: Imprenta de la Viuda de Antonio Bordazar, 1751.

Shryock, Richard H. *Medical Licensing in America, 1650–1965.* Baltimore: The Johns Hopkins Press, 1967.

Index

Index

142

Index

De la Torre household, 77–80;
scalded and beaten, 79
Froben, Johann: circle of, 33

Galán, Juan, 62–63, 78; and
Hernando de Nava, 61–62
Galeote, Alonso, 50 n. 16, 66 n. 55
Galeote, Gonzalo (the grand-
father), 50 n. 16
Galeote, Gonzalo, 51–52, 53, 55, 57,
62, 63, 66, 74–77; and attack
upon Cetina, 47, 50; and
Dominican monastery, 62, 65
"Galeotillo." *See* Galeote, Gonzalo
Gaona, Juan de, 28
Greenleaf, Richard E., 23–24 n. 1
Griego, Manuel, 23–24 n. 1, 25, 42
Grijalva, Juan de, 50 n. 16
Guatemala, 9
Guercio Valenciano, Pedro, 14, 16
Guitérrez, Fulano, 100
Guzmán, Nuño de, 95

Hernández, Francisco, 23, 24, 26,
30
Hernández de Nava, Bartolomé,
43
Hojacastro, Martín Sarmiento
de: as bishop of Tlaxcala, 4,
27 n. 12, 28, 74, 95; and Pedro de
la Torre, 38, 40
Hojeda, Cristóbal de, 8
Hojeda, Diego de, 75 n. 68, 76
Honduras, 9, 30
Honor: in the Cetina case, 52,
58–60, 70
Hospital de Desamparados, 18
n. 35

Icaza, Francisco A. de, 44 n, 97;
accepts De la Torre as legitimate doctor, 98
Indians, 16, 44; sufferings of, in
epidemics, 17, 18
Inquisition, 4, 19 n, 93, 97; and
charges of bigamy, 26, 32;
episcopal, 4, 27 n. 13

Instituto de Estudios Históricos
(Puebla), 100 n
Italy, 4, 13

Jiménez de Quesada, Gonzalo, 3, 8
Jonson, Ben, 4

Lérida, University of, 11, 14 n. 22
Licensing: of doctors, 6–7 n. 2
Logroño. 3, 28, 37
Lombardy, 4, 13
López, Dr. Pedro, 18 n. 35, 87 n. 96
López, Gonzalo, 46 n. 6, 53
López, Licentiate Pero, 8; and
De la Torre, 17; wealth of, 15,
18–19
Luisa (slave), 26, 94; and mar-
riage to De la Torre, 31, 32
Luther, Martin, 34

Madrid, 20
Mafra, Martín de, 62, 74, 75 n. 68,
76, 77, 78, 80; and attack upon
Cetina, 47, 75
Magdalena, 8
Mallaybia, Martín de, 17
Mancilla, Luis, 36
Mansilla, Fulano, 75 n. 68, 76
María, 70
Martellozzo Forin, Dr. Elda, 91 n
Martín, Antón, 48
Martínez, Alonso, 66–67 n. 56, 69,
70; and Cetina case, 56–57;
smokes out tower of Dominican
monastery, 64–65
Medical examiners. See *Proto-
médicos*
Medical titles: foreign and
Spanish, 11
Medicine: first American
doctor's degree in, 86–87 n. 96
Medina, José Toribio, 23–24 n. 1
Mejía, Dr. Antonio, 65 n. 52,
67 n. 56, 84, 85, 87; and Nava
case, 66–70
Méndez, Dr. Cristóbal, 15; criti-

143

Index

cized, 19; arraigned by the
episcopal Inquisition, 19 n
Mendoza, Viceroy Antonio de, 4,
10, 13, 14 n. 18, 20, 37
Menéndez y Pelayo, Marcelino,
44 n, 54 n. 23, 63
Mexico: mortality in, 7; Royal
and Pontifical University of,
86
Mexico City: *cabildo* of, and
legislation against curers, 7;
epidemic of smallpox in, 7;
scarcity of doctors in, 7, 9, 97
Molina, Andrés, 46
Molina, Dr. Fulano, 9, 32
Montezuma, 5
Moreno, Pedro, 9, 55, 66–67 n. 56
Motolinía, Toribio de, 27 n. 12

Narváez, Pánfilo de, 43, 66 n. 55
Nava, Ana de, 52
Nava, Hernando de, 43, 50, 52, 55,
57, 59–60, 62, 65, 66, 70 n. 64, 72,
74, 79, 81, 99, 100; and attack on
Cetina, 51, 56; character of, 53,
83; escape of, 56, 75–77; plots
against Madame de la Torre,
60, 77; invades house of Dr. de
la Torre, 60–63; wounds
Madame de la Torre, 61; takes
sanctuary in Dominican
monastery, 62; judges in case
of, 66–67 n. 56; faction of, 67;
apprehended, 68; defense of,
69; sentenced, 84; appeals to
royal *audiencia*, 84–85; jailed
in Mexico City, 85; right hand
of, amputated, 86; cost of
defense of, 88; escapes beheading, 87–88
Necromancy, 31, 93
Negroes, 16, 44, 61; sufferings of,
in epidemics, 17, 18, 27
Negro slaves. *See* Slaves, Negro

Oliver, Antonio de, 17
Osma, Leonor de, 33, 44, 53–54

n. 22, 65 n. 2, 66, 70, 72, 78, 80,
81–82, 94; as spouse of De la
Torre, 26, 43; illiteracy of, 52–53;
slashed by Hernando de Nava,
61

Padua, 8, 34; University of, 3,
11, 12, 20, 28, 90–91
Páez, Pedro, 74, 75
Pánuco, 43
Parra Cala, Rosario, 44 n
Parroquia del Sagrario
Metropolitano de Puebla, 100 n
Peralta, Francisco de, 46, 47, 48,
50, 55, 66–67 n. 56, 70 n. 64, 72,
74, 80, 81; and Madame de la
Torre, 52; urbanity of, 53–54;
takes sanctuary, 57; refuses to
involve Cetina, 59
Pérez, Francisco, 42
Pérez de Sandoval, Alonso, 9, 10;
and defense of Pedro de la
Torre, 16–17
Physicians. *See* Doctors
Plaza y Jaén, Cristóbal Bernardo
de la, 86–87 n. 96
Poor, medical care of, 19 n
Protomedicato, 97, 98
Protomédicos, 6, 7, 8, 13
Puebla de los Angeles, 4, 9, 27, 37

Ramírez, Leonor, 63, 95
Reynoso, Francisco de, 75 n. 68,
76
Roca, Lázaro de, 53–54, 70 n. 64, 81
Rodríguez Marín, Francisco, 44 n,
88 n. 100
Rodríguez, Surgeon Gaspar: and
Cetina, 57
Romero, Vicar Bartolomé, 9,
24–25; and Pedro de la Torre,
30
Rosetti, Lucia, 91 n
Ruiz, Antonio, 30
Ruiz de Rojas, Juan, 85

144

Index

145

DATE DUE

DEMCO 38-297